How to Use This Book

Look for these special features in this book:

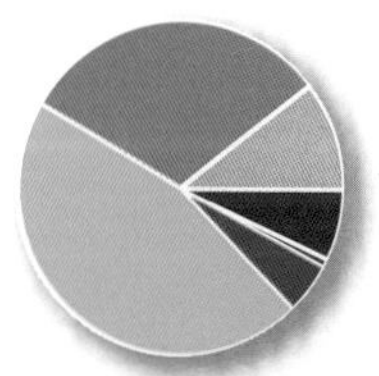

SIDEBARS, **CHARTS**, **GRAPHS**, and original **MAPS** expand your understanding of what's being discussed—and also make useful sources for classroom reports.

FAQs answer common **F**requently **A**sked **Q**uestions about people, places, and things.

WOW FACTORS offer "Who knew?" facts to keep you thinking.

TRAVEL GUIDE gives you tips on exploring the area—either in person or right from your chair!

PROJECT ROOM provides fun ideas for school assignments and incredible research projects. Plus, there's a guide to primary sources—what they are and how to cite them.

Please note: All statistics are as up-to-date as possible at the time of publication. Population data is taken from the 2010 census.

Consultants: Frank Guridy, Professor of History, University of Texas–Austin; William Loren Katz; Hernan Santos, Professor of Geology, University of Puerto Rico; Milagros Denis-Rosario, PhD, Assistant Professor, Hunter College, City University of New York

Book production by The Design Lab

Library of Congress Cataloging-in-Publication Data
Stille, Darlene R.
Puerto Rico / by Darlene R. Stille. — Revised edition.
pages cm. — (America the beautiful, third series)
Includes bibliographical references and index.
Audience: Ages 9–12.
ISBN 978-0-531-28290-8 (library binding : alk. paper)
1. Puerto Rico—Juvenile literature. I. Title.
F1958.3.S85 2014
972.95—dc23 2013044805

Printed in the United States of America 141

1 2 3 4 5 6 7 8 9 10 R 24 23 22 21 20 19 18 17 16 15

Puerto Rico

BY DARLENE R. STILLE

Third Series, Revised Edition

Children's Press®
An Imprint of Scholastic Inc.
New York ★ Toronto ★ London ★ Auckland ★ Sydney
Mexico City ★ New Delhi ★ Hong Kong
Danbury, Connecticut

CONTENTS

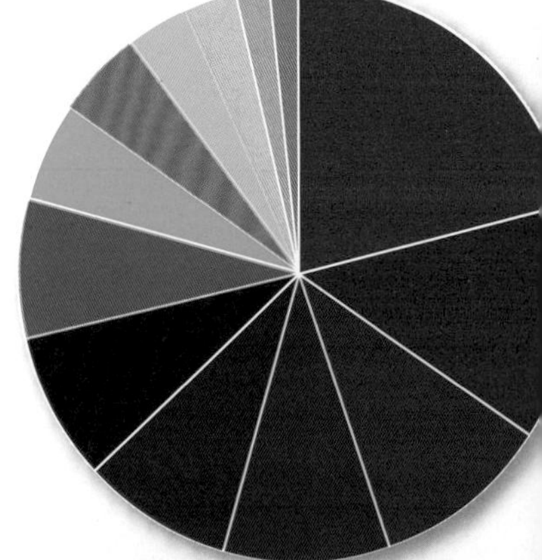

ATLANTIC OCEAN

Arecibo Observatory
Arecibo Lighthouse and Historical Park
San Cristóbal Fort
SAN JUAN
El Yunque National Forest
ARECIBO
BAYAMÓN
Culebra Island
Caguana Indian Ceremonial Park
Arecibo
Manatí
La Plata
Loíza
CAROLINA
Mona Passage
Añasco
PUERTO RICO
MAYAGÜEZ
Tres Picachos
CAGUAS
Vieques Passage
Vieques Sound
Cordillera Central
Vieques Island
PONCE
Las Cabezas de San Juan State Park
Cartagena Lagoon Natural Reserve
Caja de Muertos
Parque de Las Ciencias Luis A. Ferré
Ponce Museum of Art
Cabo Rojo Lighthouse
MUSEO

QUICK FACTS

Capital: San Juan
Largest city: San Juan
Total area: 5,325 square miles (13,792 sq km)
Highest point: Cerro de Punta, 4,390 feet (1,338 m)
Lowest point: Sea level along the Caribbean Sea

CARIBBEAN SEA

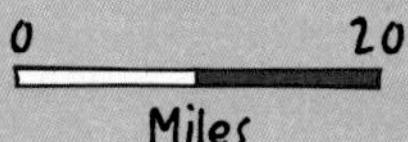

ATLANTIC OCEAN

Welcome to Puerto Rico!

HOW DID PUERTO RICO GET ITS NAME?

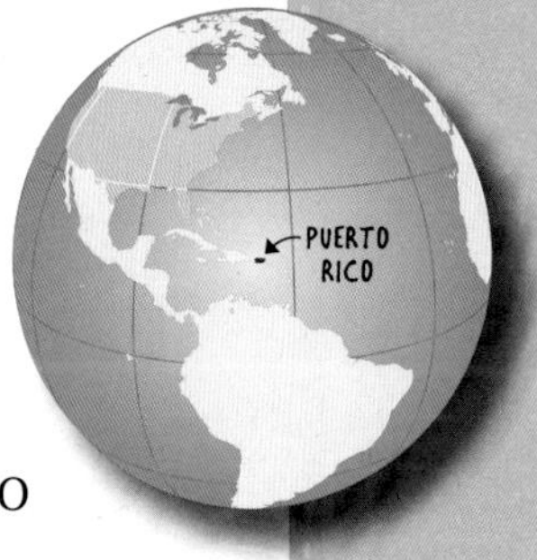

PUERTO RICO

When Christopher Columbus landed in Puerto Rico in 1493, the Native people who came to greet him called the island *Borikén* or *Borinquen*, which means "land of the brave people." Columbus gave the island a Spanish name, *San Juan Bautista* (Saint John the Baptist). The Spanish settlers who followed built a city on the north coast and named it *Puerto Rico*, meaning "rich port." Over time, the names of the city and the island were switched.

VIRGIN ISLANDS (U.K.)

VIRGIN ISLANDS (U.S.)

Anguilla

St. Martin

ST. KITTS & NEVIS

CARIBBEAN SEA

READ ABOUT

A waterfall in El Yunque National Forest

LAND

★

PUERTO RICO HAS HUNDREDS OF MILES OF BEACHES ALONG THE ATLANTIC OCEAN AND CARIBBEAN SEA. Inland, the island contains rugged mountains and deep valleys. The highest point is Cerro de Punta at 4,390 feet (1,338 meters) above sea level. The lowest point is sea level on the beaches. Though the tropical forests that once covered Puerto Rico have long since been replaced by sugar plantations, coffee trees, and many fruit trees, the island's 5,325 square miles (13,792 square kilometers) still support tropical life such as orchids and monkeys.

A view of Martinique and other islands of the West Indies

The Puerto Rico Trench is the deepest part of the Atlantic Ocean, plunging more than 5 miles (8 km). It lies about 100 miles (161 km) north of Puerto Rico and is more than 1,000 miles (1,609 km) long and about 60 miles (97 km) wide.

BUILDING MOUNTAINS

Puerto Rico is part of the West Indies, a chain of islands that runs from Florida to the tip of South America. A group of islands called the Greater Antilles marks the northern boundary of the Caribbean Sea. Puerto Rico is the smallest of four main islands in the Greater Antilles. The others are Cuba, Jamaica, and Hispaniola.

Puerto Rico and these other islands are actually the tops of mountains that stick up above the ocean waters. This undersea mountain range began forming as long as 100 million years ago. The tops of the mountains are now the West Indies.

Puerto Rico Topography

Use the color-coded elevation chart to see on the map Puerto Rico's high points (dark red to orange) and low points (green to dark green). Elevation is measured as the distance above or below sea level.

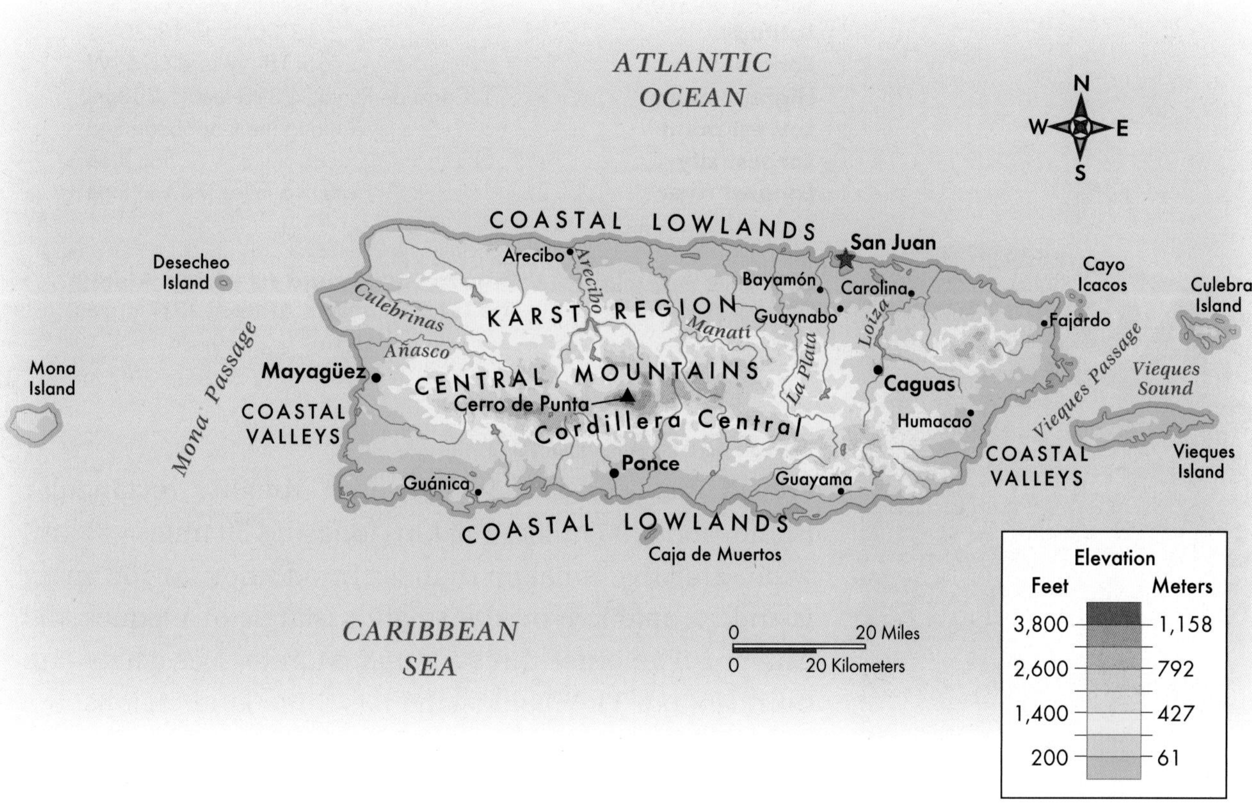

Two complex processes formed the mountains. Gigantic plates that make up the upper layer have been slowly but constantly moving around on a layer of hot, molten rock beneath. As these plates crashed together over millions of years, their edges crumpled to form mountains. Volcanoes also helped form the West Indies. Some of its islands are actually the tops of volcanoes.

Puerto Rico Geo-Facts

Total area	5,325 square miles (13,792 sq km)
Land	3,424 square miles (8,868 sq km)
Water	1,901 square miles (4,924 sq km)
Inland water	68 square miles (176 sq km)
Coastal water	16 square miles (41 sq km)
Territorial water	1,817 square miles (4,707 sq km)
Latitude	18°00' N to 18°30' N
Longitude	65°15' W to 67°15' W
Highest point	Cerro de Punta, 4,390 feet (1,338 m)
Lowest point	Sea level along the Caribbean Sea
Largest city	San Juan
Longest river	Plata, 46 miles (74 km) long

Source: U.S. Census Bureau, 2010 census

Puerto Rico could fit inside Alaska, the largest state, almost 125 times.

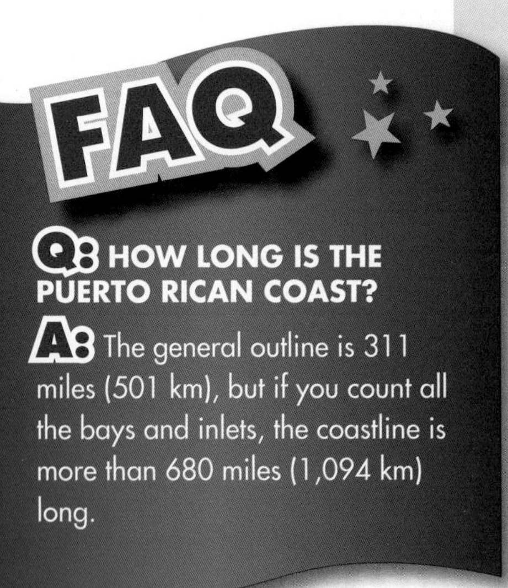

Q8 HOW LONG IS THE PUERTO RICAN COAST?

A8 The general outline is 311 miles (501 km), but if you count all the bays and inlets, the coastline is more than 680 miles (1,094 km) long.

WORDS TO KNOW

karst *limestone regions that feature many caves and sinkholes*

erosion *the gradual wearing away of rock or soil by physical breakdown, chemical solution, or water*

LAND REGIONS

Puerto Rico consists of one large, roughly rectangular island, about 90 miles (145 km) long and 30 miles (48 km) wide, and five smaller islands. In addition to the main island, people live on the smaller islands of Vieques and Culebra. The other three—Mona, Monito, Desecheo—are uninhabited. The main island has three land regions: the Central Mountains, the **Karst** Region, and the Coastal Lowlands.

Central Mountains

Several mountain ranges cross the island from east to west. The largest range, the Cordillera Central, contains Puerto Rico's highest peak, Cerro de Punta. The other ranges are the Sierra de Luquillo in the northeast, the Sierra de Cayey in the east, and the Sierra Bermeja in the southwest. Valleys between the mountains are filled with soil created from weathering and **erosion** of rocks

The Central Mountains area provides fertile soil for farming.

and other material that washed down the mountainsides. Farmers can grow crops in this soil.

Karst Region

This region lies among lower limestone hills on the northern side of the Central Mountains. Over millions of years, rainwater running over and through the limestone hills dissolved parts of the rock to form underground rivers and huge caves. Karst areas are riddled with caves, sinkholes, and humplike hills.

Coastal Lowlands

The Coastal Lowlands are a narrow strip of plains along Puerto Rico's north and south coasts. Puerto Rico's cities and beach resort areas are mainly in the northern lowlands. Pastel-colored houses and modern office buildings stretch inward from the coast. High-rise hotels line the

Espíritu Santo River, which flows in eastern Puerto Rico, is the only river on the island deep enough for boats to travel on.

land along the beaches. At 8 to 12 miles (13 to 19 km) wide, the northern lowlands are wider than the southern lowlands. Valleys extend inland from the north coast, following about 50 shallow rivers. Among the largest rivers flowing north into the Atlantic Ocean are the 46-mile-long (74 km) Plata, the 40-mile-long (64 km) Rio Grande de Loíza, and the 34-mile-long (55 km) Arecibo. Rivers flowing south into the Caribbean are dry for much of the year.

CLIMATE

You will never need to wear a winter coat in Puerto Rico, but you should keep an umbrella handy. Puerto Rico's weather is typical of a tropical climate, warm enough to go swimming all year long but sometimes very rainy. Temperatures vary slightly around the island, and there are some differences between the seasons. The average high temperature on the north coast, where most people live, is about 83 degrees Fahrenheit (28 degrees Celsius) in July and about 78°F (26°C) in January.

Boats crashed onto shore during Hurricane Georges, which hit Puerto Rico in 1998.

Weather Report

This chart shows record temperatures (high and low) for the commonwealth, as well as average temperatures (July and January) and average annual precipitation.

Record high temperature . . . . 104°F (40°C) at Mona Island on July 2, 1966
Record low temperature . . . . .40°F (4°C) at Aibonito on March 9, 1911, at San Sebastián on January 24, 1966, and at Rincón on March 27, 1985
Average July temperature, San Juan . . . . 83°F (28°C)
Average January temperature, San Juan . . . . 78°F (26°C)
Average yearly precipitation, San Juan . . . . 56 inches (142 cm)

Source: National Climatic Data Center, NESDIS, NOAA, U.S. Dept. of Commerce

Another difference between seasons is rainfall. From May to October is Puerto Rico's rainy season, but more rain falls in the northern part of the island than in the south. The north part of Puerto Rico gets an average of 60 inches (152 centimeters) a year, while parts of the south coast get about half that amount. The wettest place is El Yunque **rain forest** in the northeast, which gets up to 240 inches (610 cm) of rainfall a year!

Puerto Rico has one great weather hazard: hurricanes. These big, swirling storms form over warm ocean waters and pack winds that sometimes reach 200 miles (322 km) per hour. The winds can blow the roofs off of houses and whip up high waves that can toss boats from their water moorings onto land. Heavy rainfall from a hurricane can also cause mudslides in mountainous areas. The U.S. National Weather Service issues warnings when there is danger of a hurricane striking Puerto Rico.

HURRICANE GEORGES

In September 1998, Hurricane Georges, one of the most damaging hurricanes ever to strike Puerto Rico, ripped across the island from east to west. The hurricane leveled houses, destroyed crops, toppled power lines, and dumped so much rain that rivers overflowed their banks, washing away roads and bridges. The hurricane damaged or destroyed more than 80,000 homes and caused more than $2 billion in damages.

WORD TO KNOW

rain forest *a dense forest of broad-leaved trees, usually found in warm, wet areas*

Puerto Rico National Park Areas

This map shows some of Puerto Rico's national parks, monuments, preserves, and other areas protected by the National Park Service.

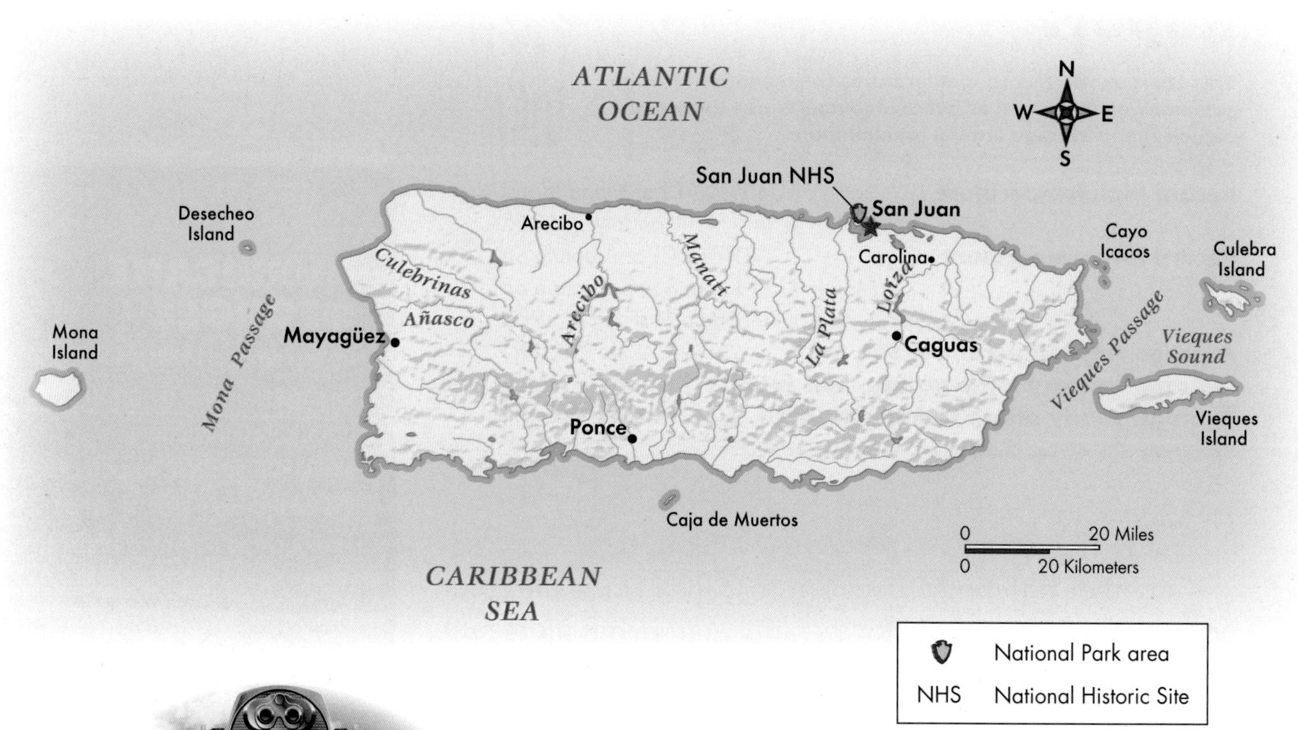

ATLANTIC OCEAN
N
W
E
S
San Juan NHS
San Juan
Desecheo Island
Arecibo
Cayo Icacos
Culebra Island
Carolina
Culebrinas
Manatí
Loíza
Arecibo
Añasco
La Plata
Mona Island
Mayagüez
Caguas
Vieques Passage
Vieques Sound
Mona Passage
Ponce
Vieques Island
Caja de Muertos
0 20 Miles
0 20 Kilometers
CARIBBEAN SEA

⛉	National Park area
NHS	National Historic Site

SEE IT HERE!

EL YUNQUE NATIONAL FOREST

El Yunque is home to thousands of species of insects, reptiles, amphibians, mammals, and plants. You can hike trails to see beautiful waterfalls, listen to the chorus of tiny tree frogs, and—if you are lucky—glimpse the rare Puerto Rican parrot. El Yunque is the only tropical rain forest under the protection of the U.S. Forest Service's National Forest system. It covers 28,000 acres (11,330 hectares) near San Juan and was formerly known as the Caribbean National Forest.

PLANT LIFE

Most of Puerto Rico's original rain forest is gone, but there are still beautiful plants everywhere in Puerto Rico. El Yunque National Forest is home to fern trees and about 50 species of orchids, some of the few plant species left that are native to Puerto Rico. Puerto Rico's orchids grow mainly on the trunks and branches of trees and produce purple, white, pink, or yellow blossoms. Explorers and settlers

A flowering African tulip tree in El Yunque National Forest

from other parts of the world brought many plant species, such as breadfruit and coconut palms. Various species of green plants carpet the hillsides and mountains. The African tulip tree and the royal poinciana, also called the flamboyant tree, grow blossoms that from a distance look like red or orange pom-poms.

A hummingbird feeding on a banana blossom

ANIMAL LIFE

Most of Puerto Rico's wildlife lives in protected areas, such as El Yunque National Forest. On a hike through the rain forest, you will not see any large wild mammals, because none ever lived on the island. Bats are the only surviving land mammals that are native to Puerto Rico. But you might see small mammals that came to the island on sailing ships, such as long, thin mongooses from Asia. Mongooses were used to kill rats on sugar plantations.

Coqui

Hikers in Puerto Rico's rain forest do not have to worry about startling a poisonous snake, because there are none on the island. Puerto Rico does not have many snakes at all, but there are iguanas, anoles, and other types of lizards. At night, you may hear Puerto Rico's beloved coqui, a tiny frog whose name sounds like its call, "co-kee." There are also countless insects, including flies, beetles, and many kinds of moths.

Puerto Rico is a good place to watch tropical birds. The island is home to more than 200 bird species, from the rare Puerto Rican parrot to the tiny but colorful tody. The sea around Puerto Rico is filled with all kinds of marine animals, including barracudas, sharks, dolphins, whales, and many types of tropical fish.

A school of fish along a coral reef off the shore of Guánica

A Puerto Rican parrot living in El Yunque National Forest

ENDANGERED SPECIES

The U.S. government includes dozens of plants and animals in Puerto Rico on the endangered or threatened species list. The Puerto Rican parrot is one. This beautiful bird grows to about 12 inches (30 cm) long. It has a bright green body, red on its forehead, and white rings around its eyes. Scientists estimate that there could have been as many as 1 million Puerto Rican parrots when Europeans first arrived on the island in 1493. By 2006, only 200 remained, and only about 30 of these lived in the wild in El Yunque National Forest. The U.S. government and the Puerto Rico Department of Natural and Environmental Resources are breeding the birds in captivity and hope to release them back into the rain forest. If they can get about 500 parrots to live in the wild, they think the species may survive.

HUMANS AND THE ENVIRONMENT

Since the 1500s, humans have had a tremendous impact on Puerto Rico's island environment. Soon after the first Europeans arrived, they began cutting down trees. The rate at which Europeans destroyed the rain forest increased over the centuries. In the 1700s, they cleared hundreds of thousands of trees to make way for sugarcane, coffee, and tobacco crops. Huge plantations replaced much of the rain forest. In the 1800s and early 1900s, loggers cut more trees for lumber and firewood.

In the mid-1900s, world demand for Puerto Rico's sugarcane dropped, and planters abandoned some fields. Trees and other rain forest plants began to grow again. **Botanists** call trees and other plants that replace the

WORD TO KNOW

botanists *scientists who study plants*

When people clear trees from Puerto Rico's rain forests, they often destroy the homes of many plants and animals.

original forest "secondary growth." The species of trees that were planted, including palm and mahogany, were not native to Puerto Rico. Explorers and settlers had brought them to the island. Many of Puerto Rico's native animals and plants were wiped out or became endangered, mainly because their rain forest homes were destroyed.

One of the greatest environmental challenges faced by Puerto Ricans is how to preserve the island's remaining rain forests. Both government and private researchers are looking at ways to do this using secondary growth. In a 1,010-acre (409 ha) rain forest on the steep mountains of southeastern Puerto Rico, they have planted mahogany and other hardwood trees that make good lumber. The forest researchers are also studying how many trees can be cut without harming the forest and causing erosion. If loggers cut down all the trees, rainwater will run down the mountainsides, erode the soil, and carry pollutants, such as wastes from cows, pigs, and other livestock on nearby farms, into the streams and rivers below.

The government is also limiting access to some of the rain forest, so it can thrive in its natural state. In 2005, the U.S. Congress protected 10,000 acres (4,047 ha), about half of El Yunque National Forest, as the El Toro Wilderness Area. No logging, mining, or motor vehicles are allowed in a wilderness area. To visit the El Toro section of El Yunque, you have to hike or ride a horse.

AGUSTÍN STAHL: RECORDER OF PUERTO RICAN PLANTS

Agustín Stahl (1842–1917) was born in Aguadilla, trained as a doctor in Europe, and then returned home to practice medicine. Stahl loved nature and traveled all over Puerto Rico collecting plant specimens, writing about them, and painting watercolors showing what the plants look like. Many botanists have used his writings and pictures to do further studies.

La Mina Falls in El Yunque National Forest plunges some 35 feet (11 m) into a pool of water.

READ ABOUT

A Taíno drawing from the Caguana Ceremonial Ball Courts Site

c. 7000–3000 BCE
Casimiroid people arrive from Central America

c. 2000 BCE
Ortoiroid people arrive from South America

▲c. 500 BCE
The Saladoid culture grows cassava (above) and makes pottery

FIRST PEOPLE

★

IMAGINE WALKING FROM CENTRAL AMERICA TO PUERTO RICO. Experts suspect that is how some Native Americans arrived on the island. The water level of the Caribbean Sea used to be much lower than it is now, and a " land bridge" may have connected Central America to the mountains that became the islands of the West Indies. People in Central America may have begun to journey over the bridge as long as 9,000 years ago.

c. 600 CE
The Ostionoid culture builds plazas and ball courts

c. 800
Arawak/Taíno people begin arriving

Late 1400s ►
Caribs raid Taíno villages

Archaeologist Hernan Bustelo studies ancient stones at a site in Ponce.

THE FIRST PUERTO RICANS

Archaeologists call the people who walked to what are now Jamaica, Cuba, Hispaniola, and western Puerto Rico the Casimiroid people. Scientists who studied ancient campsites on Mona Island and the western main island found bone spear tips, stone axes, and other tools with decorations on them. Casimiroids may have been hunter-gatherers who lived mainly on shellfish and small animals.

In about 2000 BCE, another group set out from South America in canoes. Archaeologists call the people who arrived by canoe the Ortoiroid people. Scientists have found tools and other evidence of these hunter-gatherers everywhere in Puerto Rico, from the coast to the mountains.

WORD TO KNOW

archaeologists *people who study the remains of past human societies*

Native American Peoples

(Before European Contact)

This map shows the general area of Native American peoples before European settlers arrived.

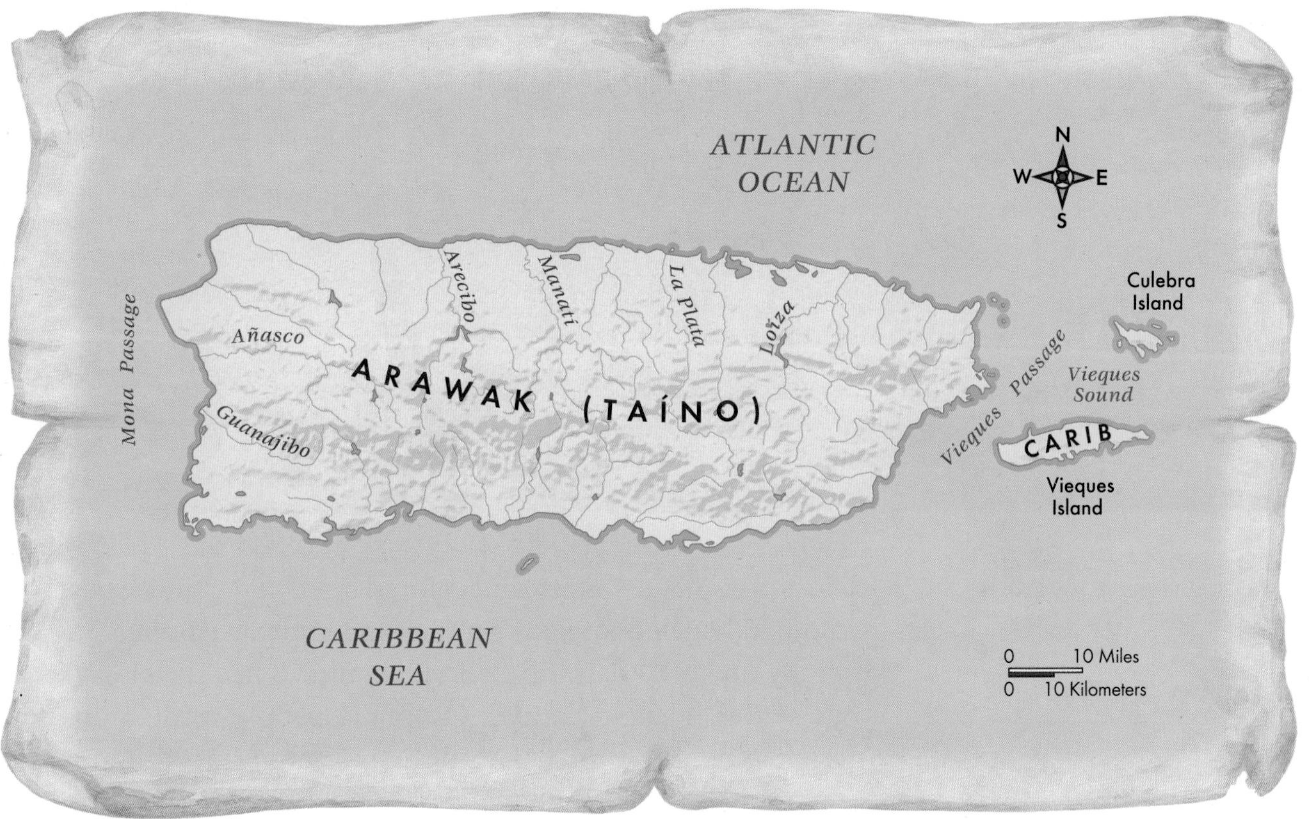

The Casimiroid people decorated their tools, but the Ortoiroid people did not.

THE POTTERY MAKERS

About 2,500 years ago, a group of people left the northeast coast of South America and headed north across the Atlantic Ocean to the islands of the Caribbean Sea. Archaeologists call these people the Saladoid culture. Saladoids brought new skills to Puerto Rico. They had

This stone circle at a site called Caguana is believed to have been a Taíno ball court.

learned to make pottery and colored it red and white. They also had learned to plant some crops, such as **cassava**.

By about 600 CE, the Ostionoid culture had developed out of the Saladoid culture. Ostionoid people made a different type of pottery, with designs carved into it. More important, Ostionoid people developed a society that built villages with central plazas and ball courts.

WORD TO KNOW

cassava *a starchy tropical root that looks somewhat like a big carrot*

Cassava

THE ARAWAK PEOPLE

Meanwhile, the Arawak civilization was developing in the Andes Mountains of eastern South America. As the number of Arawaks grew, they began to spread out, first along the Amazon River, then along the Orinoco. Finally, they set out in canoes to settle the islands of the Caribbean.

Arawaks were a peaceful people. They lived in villages, fished, and planted corn, cassava, gourds, and other crops. Arawaks brought their civilization to many Caribbean islands, and each island developed its own society. But they all spoke the Arawakan language.

Several English words come from the Arawakan language, such as barbecue, from *barbacoa*, hammock from *hamaca*, canoe from *kanoa*, tobacco from *tabaco*, and hurricane from *hurakan*.

MOUND FARMING

Arawaks began settling in Puerto Rico around 800. Those who settled in Puerto Rico are called Taínos. They cut down the rain forest trees to build houses and make room for villages and farm fields. They burned the trees and other plants to make more space, and kept the ashes, which helped to fertilize the soil. Taínos piled soil and ashes into cone-shaped mounds and planted food crops, cotton, and tobacco. They also hunted and ate fish and small animals.

This exhibit shows how a Taíno village may have appeared.

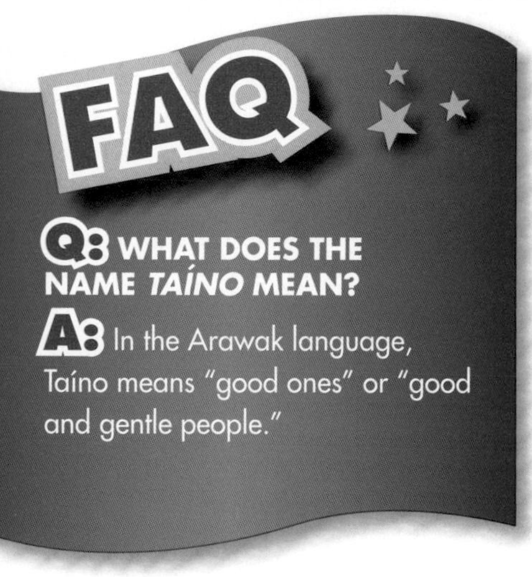

Q8 WHAT DOES THE NAME *TAÍNO* MEAN?

A8 In the Arawak language, Taíno means "good ones" or "good and gentle people."

NOBLES AND WORKERS

Through farming, fishing, and hunting, the Taíno people could easily feed themselves. They had abundant spare time to spend on religious ceremonies. They also developed a complex society, which had two basic classes: nobles and common people. From the noble class came leaders, or *caciques*, and medicine men, or *bohiques*. A cacique, who was also a spiritual leader, ruled over a settlement that could have between several hundred and several thousand people. The island was divided among 20 caciques. The bohiques communicated with Taíno nature gods and advised the caciques about when to hold ceremonies or go to war. The common people did all the work of the village.

Most Taínos lived in round houses made of wooden frames covered with plant leaves and topped with cone-

SEE IT HERE!

PUERTO RICO INDIAN MUSEUM

The Puerto Rico Indian Museum in San Juan is a small museum packed with many artifacts that archaeologists dug up—the ancient objects that Taínos used in their daily lives, including pottery, carved nature gods called *cemis* or *zemis*, and body ornaments. Exhibits show how Taínos lived and even show one of the canoes they used. The Puerto Rico Institute of Culture created the museum to present an introduction to the history and culture of these early Puerto Ricans.

A Taíno cacique being carried on a raised platform

Petroglyphs from the Taíno people

shaped **thatch** roofs. These dwellings were called *bohios*. The cacique's house was rectangular and larger than other people's houses. Most caciques were men, but women could also be caciques. A male cacique could have as many as 30 wives.

Men and women did different jobs in the village. In the stillness and dim light of the dense rain forest, men stalked small mammals, lizards, and other animals. They cast lines and nets in the rivers to catch fish and hunted for ducks and turtles. Women cooked the fish and meat, planted seeds in the big farm mounds, harvested the crops, and made bread from ground cassava.

Taínos made pottery for cooking and storing food, and they carved wood or stone into images that represented their nature gods. They created records by carving pictures or symbols called **petroglyphs** into rocks. Out of wood, Taínos carved chairs with high backs and short legs. The

WOW

In 2007, archaeologists uncovered a huge plaza surrounded by stones engraved with petroglyphs. It may have been a major Taíno settlement in southern Puerto Rico.

WORDS TO KNOW

thatch *a roof covering made of straw, palm leaves, or other plant material*

petroglyphs *pictures carved or painted on stone*

Picture Yourself . . .

at a Taíno Ceremony

Excitement fills the air as you wake up in the morning. Today, there will be a ceremony in the plaza. You get dressed up by decorating your body with colorful paint made from plants or minerals. You put on jewelry made of beautifully carved bone or shells. Your parents are also preparing for the ceremony. They paint their bodies and wear jewelry, feathers, or other ornaments. Your mother wears a kind of apron around her waist.

Now it is time for the ceremony to begin. The whole village gathers around the plaza to watch as the cacique is carried in on a carved chair, wearing a gold medallion around his neck. Musicians pound drums and play flutes and other instruments. People dance. Then the cacique sings songs about heroes and great events of long ago. Best of all, there is a wonderful feast.

cacique sat on one of these chairs during public ceremonies.

CEREMONIES AND BALL GAMES

Ceremonies were very important to the Taíno people. The ceremonies were held for many reasons, such as celebrating the wedding of a noble or a visit from an important person, or to give thanks for a good harvest. All ceremonies were held in the central plaza of the village. The cacique played a big part by singing songs that told about the ancestors and the history of the Taíno people.

Just as important as ceremonies was a ball game called *batey*. This game was a lot like soccer. Two teams of at least 12 people each tried to get a hard rubber ball into the opposing team's goal. Players could hit the ball with their head, feet, arms, legs, elbows, or hips—any body part except their hands. They could also hit the ball with a carved stone belt worn around the waist. Both men and women played batey, and they wore cotton padding around their arms and legs to keep from being hurt by the hard, fast-moving ball.

Taíno shell necklace

WORD TO KNOW

anthropologists *people who study the development of human cultures*

The ball game and other customs of the Taíno people were similar to customs of other Native groups, such as the Maya people of Central America. Because of their similar customs, **anthropologists** and archaeologists think that Taínos traded and visited with people on other islands and the mainland. Taínos were good sailors and built sturdy dugout canoes from trees. They hollowed out the inside of the tree by setting small fires, then scraping away the charred wood. They used huge trees to make ocean-going canoes that could hold more than 100 people.

MINI-BIO

RICARDO E. ALEGRÍA: SCHOLAR OF ANCIENT PUERTO RICAN CULTURE

Born in San Juan, writer, anthropologist, and archaeologist Ricardo E. Alegría (1921–2011) was one of the first scientists to study the customs, history, and art of the Taíno people. He helped found the Institute of Puerto Rican Culture and staged museum exhibitions to display the artwork of the Taínos. Alegría correctly determined that about one-third of all Puerto Ricans are descendants of the Taínos.

Want to know more? Visit www.factsfornow.scholastic.com and enter the keywords **Puerto Rico**.

CARIBS

The Taínos' peaceful life was doomed from the late 1400s. Riding the ocean waves in big dugout war canoes came raiders from a Native group called Caribs. The Carib people, like the Arawak/Taíno people, had migrated from the Amazon rain forests of South America. Caribs first took over islands in the southern Caribbean. In the 1400s, they began raiding islands farther north, killing the men and taking the women captive. In the late 1400s, they began raiding coastal villages on Puerto Rico. It looked like just a matter of time before they would take over that island, too. But an equally bad, or perhaps worse, fate lay in store for both Taínos and Caribs.

This illustration shows a Carib man. The Carib people came to Puerto Rico in the late 1400s.

READ ABOUT

This woodcut shows Christopher Columbus in the West Indies in 1493.

1493
Christopher Columbus lands on Puerto Rico

1509 ►
Juan Ponce de León is named governor of the island

1513
The first enslaved Africans arrive in Puerto Rico

EXPLORATION AND SETTLEMENT

★

AS TAÍNOS WERE FACING CARIBS IN PUERTO RICO, EVENTS UNFOLDING IN EUROPE WOULD FOREVER CHANGE THE LIVES OF THE NATIVE PEOPLE OF THE CARIBBEAN. In 1492, Christopher Columbus, sailing from Spain, led a voyage that began a period of European exploration and conquest of the Americas. On a second voyage, in 1493, he landed on Puerto Rico. After claiming it for Spain and naming it San Juan Bautista, he left and never returned.

1539
Spaniards begin building El Morro

1598 ►
English forces capture El Morro

1625
Dutch forces burn San Juan

European Exploration of Puerto Rico

The colored arrows on this map show the route taken by Christopher Columbus between 1493 and 1496.

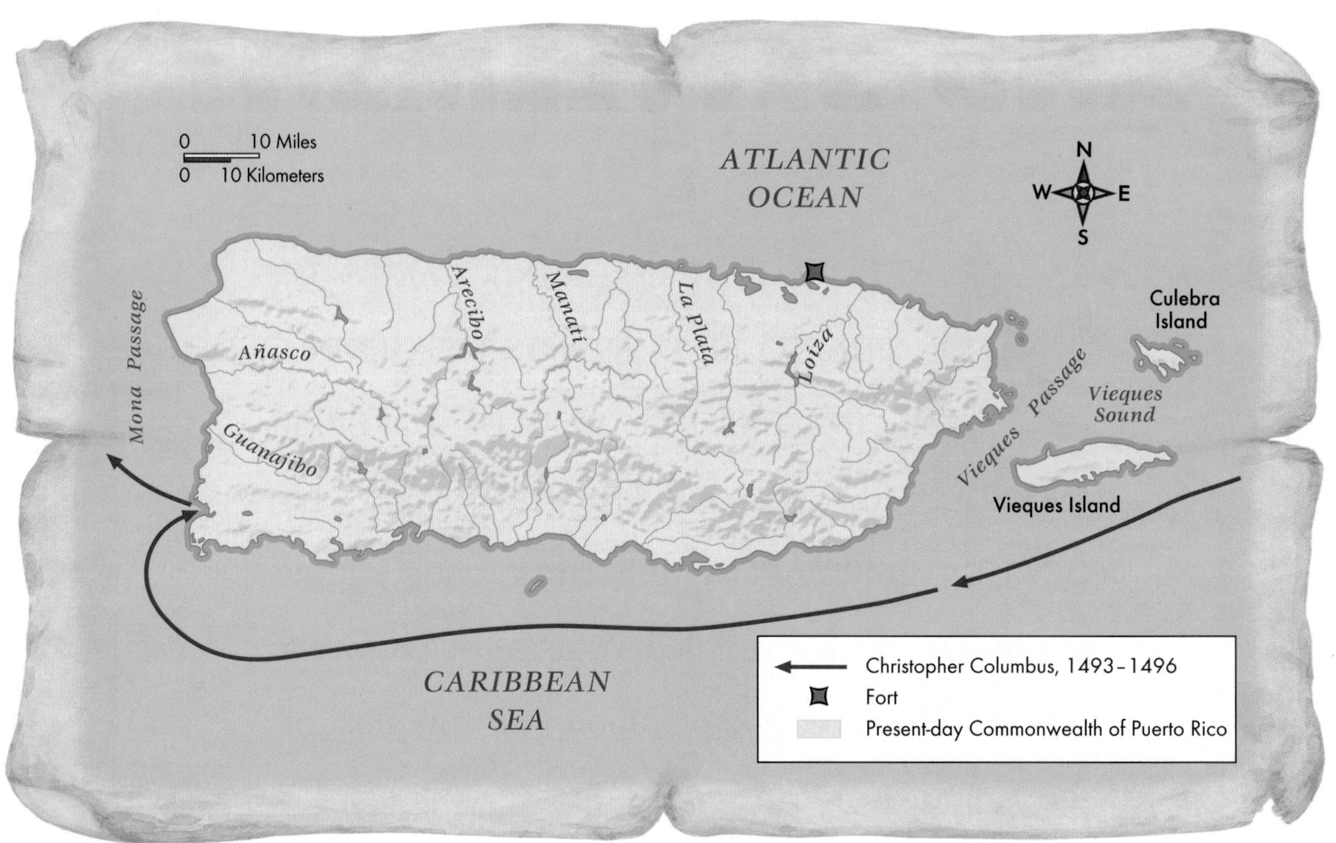

THE SPANIARDS ARRIVE

The Spaniards paid little attention to Puerto Rico and left the Taíno people alone until 1508, when a group led by Spanish **conquistador** Juan Ponce de León arrived. At that time, the leader of all the caciques was named Agüeybaná. He thought the Spaniards—with their shining armor, horses, and powerful guns—must be gods. He gave them a warm welcome, holding feasts in their honor.

WORD TO KNOW

conquistador *one who conquers; specifically a leader in the Spanish conquest of the Americas*

In a special ceremony showing friendship, he exchanged names with Ponce de León.

Agüeybaná and the friendly Taínos showed the Spaniards rivers where nuggets of gold were waiting to be picked from the water. Ponce de León wrote to the Spanish king about the gold, and the king replied, "Be very diligent in searching for gold mines in the island of San Juan; take out as much as possible." Ponce de León demanded that Taínos mine gold and clear rain forest areas for farms. The king made him governor of the island, and Ponce de León established the first Spanish colonial town, which he called Caparra.

MINI-BIO

JUAN PONCE DE LEÓN: CONQUISTADOR

Juan Ponce de León (1460–1521) was born in San Servas, Spain, and may have sailed with Columbus on his second voyage in 1493–1494. In 1509, Ponce de León became Puerto Rico's first Spanish colonial governor. King Ferdinand of Spain sent him to explore further, and in 1513 he discovered Florida. According to legend, Ponce de León was looking for a "fountain of youth" that would keep anyone who drank from it young forever. He returned to Florida in 1521 and was fatally wounded in a battle with Native Americans. Puerto Rico's fourth-largest city, Ponce, was named in his honor.

? **Want to know more?** Visit www.factsfornow.scholastic.com and enter the keywords **Puerto Rico**.

THE FATE OF THE TAÍNO PEOPLE

Agüeybaná took care not to anger the powerful Spaniards, and so there was peace while he lived. In 1510, he developed an unknown illness and died, and his brother took over. The new cacique, Agüeybaná II, did not like or trust the Spaniards. He led the Taíno people in a rebellion in 1511 and killed hundreds of Spaniards. Taínos' bows and arrows, however, were no match for Spanish guns, swords, and body armor. Spaniards killed Agüeybaná II and enslaved the Taíno people, forcing men, women, and children to work from sunrise to sunset in gold mines.

Q8 WHY DID COLUMBUS CALL TAÍNOS "INDIANS"?

A8 Columbus thought he had landed in the East Indies, a group of Pacific Ocean islands in Southeast Asia, and therefore he called the island people "Indians." Europeans began calling all Native people in the Western Hemisphere "Indians."

Spanish missionary Bartolomé de Las Casas tried to free the Taínos from slavery.

In addition to wanting gold, the rulers of Spain wanted converts to Christianity. Along with the Spanish soldiers and settlers came Roman Catholic priests to serve as **missionaries**. The missionaries were distressed by how the soldiers treated the Taíno people. They tried to persuade the rulers in Spain to stop the beating and killing. Bishop Bartolomé de Las Casas devoted his life to fighting to free Taínos from slavery and Spanish cruelty. At one point he said "the Indians were the only true Christians" in the Americas.

The foremost concern of Spain's rulers was exploiting the land. They promised that every Spaniard who came to the Americas would be allowed to bring 12 enslaved Africans. The first enslaved Africans arrived in Puerto Rico in 1513, and by 1550, there were some 15,000 on the island. By 1570, Spaniards or Caribs had killed or worked to death almost all Taínos. Many Taínos also died of diseases that the Spaniards brought with them. But some Taínos married Africans. Others married Spaniards. Their children, called **mestizos**, were of mixed Spanish and Indian heritage, and this new population of Puerto Ricans began to grow.

WORDS TO KNOW

missionaries *people who try to convert others to a religion*

mestizos *people of mixed Spanish and Indian heritage*

PIRATES AND PRIVATEERS

The sight of white sails approaching over the green-blue waters in the late 1500s could mean either Spanish **galleons** or deadly enemies. All too often, approaching ships meant enemies.

By 1550, Spain owned a rich and powerful empire that took in present-day Mexico, Central America, parts of North and South America, and most Caribbean islands. Galleons

WORD TO KNOW

galleons *heavy Spanish sailing ships from colonial times*

Spanish settlers first began bringing African slaves to Puerto Rico in 1513.

A map of Puerto Rico, dating from the late 1500s

carried gold, silver, and other riches from the colonies to Spain. The last stop before setting off across the Atlantic Ocean, and the first stop for returning galleons, was San Juan. This city was originally a settlement named San Juan Bautista de Puerto Rico, built on a tiny island in the harbor in 1521 by Spaniards who wanted to escape from mosquito-infested Caparra. The treasure ships made Puerto Rico an irresistible target for other European nations, which often attacked the harbor at San Juan.

Caribs also attacked. Spanish rulers decided they had better build more forts to protect Puerto Rico. The first fortification, La Fortaleza, was built between 1533 and 1540 to protect against Carib attacks. The island settlement at the mouth of the harbor was a logical place for more forts. In 1539, Spaniards began building a massive stone fort called El Morro. Over the years, they added more forts, including San Cristóbal and El Cañuelo.

Spain, which was a Catholic country, was at war with almost all the Protestant nations of Europe during most of the 1500s and 1600s. England and other countries also resented Spain for not allowing any other nation to trade with its colonies. With their government's blessing, British privateers looted Spanish ships. Privateers such as Sir Francis Drake and Sir John Hawkins were heroes to the British, but they were no better than pirates in the opinion of the Spanish.

Spain accused Queen Elizabeth I of doing nothing to stop the privateers. In 1588, Spain sent a fleet of about 130 warships, called the Armada, to attack England. The

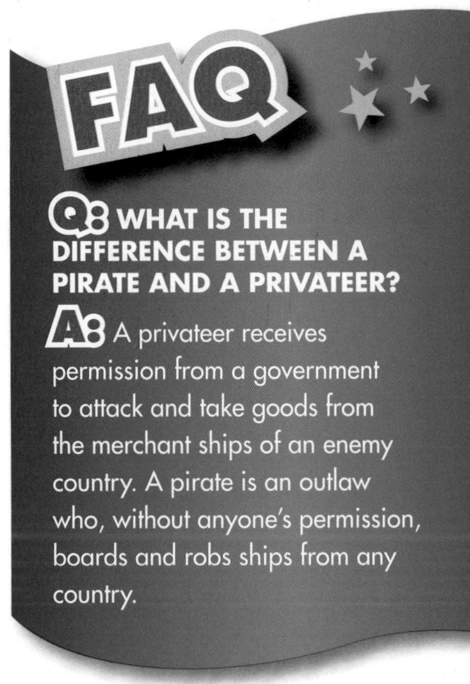

FAQ

Q8 WHAT IS THE DIFFERENCE BETWEEN A PIRATE AND A PRIVATEER?

A8 A privateer receives permission from a government to attack and take goods from the merchant ships of an enemy country. A pirate is an outlaw who, without anyone's permission, boards and robs ships from any country.

The retreat of the Spanish Armada after it was defeated by British forces in 1588

SEE IT HERE!

FORT SAN FELIPE DEL MORRO

The massive structure known as El Morro guarded the entrance to San Juan Bay when the Spanish controlled Puerto Rico. Today, it is part of San Juan National Historic Site, operated by the U.S. National Park Service. Visitors can walk through rooms and passageways with cool stone walls and look over the beautiful bay from stone towers. Construction on El Morro started in 1539 and continued for hundreds of years. The fort would grow to have six levels and walls that were 60 feet (18 m) thick.

British navy defeated the Armada, dealing a terrible blow to Spain's power and prestige. Within a few years, privateers were raiding Spanish colonies and galleons all over the Caribbean.

In 1595, Drake and Hawkins sailed with 27 ships to attack San Juan. As the British ships approached the massive walls of El Morro, the fort's big guns opened fire, driving the British away. San Juan and the soldiers in El Morro were not so fortunate in 1598, when British forces captured the fort and occupied the city. Illness soon swept through the British ranks, however, and they decided to leave because they were too weak to defend the fort.

In 1625, Dutch forces burned San Juan. Spain, by the 1700s, had lost many of its colonies in the Caribbean as the Dutch, French, British, and Danish established bases on Jamaica, Hispaniola, and other islands. Spain, however, managed to keep control of Puerto Rico.

Fort San Felipe del Morro at the entrance to San Juan Bay

AFRICANS IN PUERTO RICO

The great majority of blacks in Puerto Rico in the 1500s were enslaved Africans who were forced to clear trees, plant sugarcane, and harvest crops. But some free blacks living in Spain also settled in Puerto Rico, and some of them were put in charge of enslaved Africans.

One of Puerto Rico's first Spanish historians, Fray Íñigo Abbad y Lasierra, described how enslaved Africans were treated in Puerto Rico in the 1780s: "Some masters treat them with harshness . . . causing disloyalty, desertion and suicide; others regard them with excessive . . . affection." The Africans deeply resented their treatment and resisted slavery by trying to escape and sometimes staging rebellions.

The number of free and enslaved Africans continued to increase in Puerto Rico, because labor was needed to grow food and support the Spanish troops stationed in the forts. To increase the working population, a Spanish edict of 1664 offered free land in Puerto Rico to free Africans in Jamaica, Haiti, and other Caribbean islands not controlled by Spain.

Many enslaved Africans in Puerto Rico were able to purchase their freedom and that of their families through extra hours of labor. The Roman Catholic Church, believing all people had souls worthy of being saved, helped. Slaves could be freed by judges or in churches with the permission of their masters.

Meanwhile, Spanish and mestizo men often married African women. Their children were of mixed Spanish-

AFRICAN CONQUISTADOR

Juan Garrido (1480?–1547) had been born a prince in a kingdom in West Africa. His parents sent him to Portugal to be educated, and he later moved to Spain, where he took the name of a man he worked for. In search of adventure, he joined Ponce de León's expeditions and arrived in Puerto Rico in 1508. He was the first of many free Africans to come to Puerto Rico. He later went to Mexico, where he fought against the Aztec people. He eventually settled in Mexico City, where he lived the rest of his life.

In Puerto Rico, some marriages were between people from different ethnic groups. This illustration shows a Spanish husband with a mestizo wife.

African or Spanish-Taíno-African descent and were called mulattoes. By the 1700s, there were very few Puerto Ricans of pure Spanish descent.

THE ROLE OF CASTE

Puerto Rican society in the 1600s and 1700s was divided into **castes**, or classes. The highest caste was made up of *peninsulares*, Spaniards born in Spain. Puerto Rico's rulers were peninsulares. Below them were the *criollos*, pure-blooded Spaniards born in Puerto Rico. People of these two castes owned almost all the land in Puerto Rico and lived in fine houses called haciendas.

The lowest caste was made up of enslaved people, who supported the upper-caste way of life. *Jíbaros*, poor

WORD TO KNOW

castes *social classes that people are born into*

mulatto or mestizo farmers, ranked just higher than enslaved people. Some jíbaros worked on the plantations, and others grew crops on small pieces of land. The jíbaros grew only enough crops to feed themselves and their families. Most did not even have plows.

Throughout the 1600s and 1700s, the island remained an outpost of the Spanish Empire. Spain paid little attention to Puerto Rico beyond the harbor of San Juan and the military outpost there. To the Spanish rulers, Puerto Rico was mainly a place for ships to stop on their journeys across the Atlantic Ocean.

Picture Yourself . . .

in a Jíbaro Family

As a jíbaro child, you live in the country or in a small town with a plaza and a Catholic church. You spend your whole life in this town, never venturing through the dense rain forest to nearby villages. Your family's house, made of wood covered with palm leaves and bark, is set on poles above the ground to keep the floor dry. The house has one or two rooms. If you are a boy, you fish in nearby streams and help your father burn and chop down trees to make fields for crops. If you are a girl, you help your mother cook and make salt fish that does not rot in the hot, humid climate. You also milk the family cow. You and your brothers and sisters do not go to school, but your parents teach you the importance of being kind and honest. You attend church every Sunday and look forward to celebrating religious holidays with music and dancing.

The port of San Juan in the late 1600s

READ ABOUT

The city and harbor of Ponce, mid-1800s

1815
Spain allows Puerto Rico to begin trading with other nations

1830
Large numbers of European immigrants begin arriving in Puerto Rico

1868 ▲
Ramón Emeterio Betances helps lead the revolt at Lares

GROWTH AND CHANGE

★

FARAWAY EVENTS WERE TO AGAIN AFFECT PUERTO RICO. Colonists in North America had won independence from Great Britain in the late 1700s. In France, citizens overthrew the king. By the 1800s, these and other movements for freedom eventually brought changes to Spain and its colonies, including Puerto Rico.

1873
The Spanish government abolishes slavery

Late 1800s
Spain allows Puerto Ricans to form political parties

1898 ►
The United States takes over Puerto Rico

Followers of Miguel Hidalgo y Costilla fighting for independence in Mexico, 1810

SPAIN'S LATIN AMERICAN LOSSES

Spain, weakened by wars in Europe, lost much of its empire in the Americas. The first rebellions against Spain began in South America in 1809. Two colonial generals, Simón Bolívar and José de San Martín, led armies of patriots who won independence from Spain for Argentina, Bolivia, Chile, Colombia, Ecuador, Panama, Peru, and Venezuela. A Catholic priest, Father Miguel Hidalgo y Costilla, sparked a revolution in 1810 that led to Mexico's independence. By 1825, Spain had lost all of its possessions in the Western Hemisphere except Cuba and Puerto Rico.

MORE TRADE AND FREE LAND

Spain did not allow its colonies to manufacture goods. They had to import everything except food from Spain. Puerto Rico's colonial rulers and military depended on a type of government payment called a subsidy. Spain ordered that money for the subsidy be paid from the treasury of Mexico. Payments stopped when Mexico's war for independence broke out in 1810.

Spain feared the influence of independence movements on Puerto Rico, which had grown poorer than ever. Something had to be done to improve the situation. In 1815, Spain issued the Royal Decree of Graces, which allowed criollo Puerto Rican merchants and plantation owners to trade with countries other than Spain. It also offered free land, first to any Spaniard willing to move to Puerto Rico and then to immigrants from any Catholic country. Some Spaniards, loyal to the king of Spain and his colonial system, came to Puerto Rico from Latin American countries where revolutions had occurred.

Beginning around 1830, many European countries were experiencing economic and political problems. Waves of immigrants seeking a better life came to Puerto Rico from France, Germany, Italy, and the Mediterranean island of Corsica. Irish immigrants began to arrive in 1840, fleeing a **famine** that plagued their country.

Many newcomers used their free land to set up plantations in the interior mountains. The Corsicans established coffee plantations. The Irish became successful sugar plantation owners. The French and Italians entered the tobacco, cotton, and sugar industries. The Germans established import-export businesses in coastal towns. The newcomers learned Spanish and married local people. The population grew from 183,000 people in 1812 to about 500,000 by the mid-1800s.

WORD TO KNOW

famine *a period of extreme food shortages and hunger*

The immigrants and the plantations they set up brought new wealth to Puerto Rico. For the first time, Puerto Rico exported more goods than it imported. But the great majority of Puerto Ricans were still farmers who lived in extreme poverty.

SUGAR AND SLAVERY

Although it is impossible to farm Puerto Rico's steep mountainsides, the valleys between the interior mountains proved to be good for growing sugar. In the 1800s and early 1900s, growing, processing, and exporting sugar to the United States and other countries was Puerto Rico's main industry.

Enslaved workers cutting sugarcane in the mid-1800s

Sugar being processed on a Puerto Rican plantation

Successful sugar plantations required an enormous amount of manual labor. The need for more labor to work on the plantations brought a demand for more enslaved Africans. Before the expansion of the island's sugar industry, enslaved people in Puerto Rico had had some freedom. It was against the law to separate married couples or families, and slaves were allowed to work for money on their own time. Conditions worsened for Puerto Rico's enslaved Africans after plantation owners from other colonies arrived. As a result, there were many slave uprisings throughout Puerto Rico.

SEE IT HERE!

MUSEUM OF OUR AFRICAN ROOTS

This San Juan museum contains many exhibits about the influence of Africans on the heritage and culture of Puerto Rico. The exhibits begin with the story of Ashanti, Bantu, Congo, and Yoruba people taken from West and Central Africa and describe the hardships they experienced on the trip across the Atlantic Ocean and on the plantations. Other exhibits show the influence of folk art, religious beliefs, and music on the culture of modern Puerto Rico, including African drums used in *bomba* music.

A crowd celebrates the annual Grito de Lares festival, which honors the city's rebellion of 1868.

SEE IT HERE!

LARES

One of the most important places for the people of Puerto Rico is the little mountain city of Lares, known as the birthplace of Puerto Rico. You can stand in the spot where in 1868 a group of Puerto Ricans rebelled against Spanish rule. The town is now a historic site. The Plaza de la Revolución and a monument to the rebellion's leader, Ramón Emeterio Betances, were built here in honor of Puerto Rico's first cry for independence. In 1969, September 23 became an official holiday to commemorate the Lares rebellion.

THE CRY FOR INDEPENDENCE

As Puerto Rico's prosperity grew, so did the gap between the Spanish peninsulares, who ruled the island from San Juan, and the criollos, who operated the plantations and businesses in other parts of the country. The peninsulares used the money from crop exports to pay themselves and build up military forces on the island. They did not use it to build roads or railroads or to improve the lives of ordinary Puerto Ricans. Only about 20 percent of Puerto Ricans in the 1800s could read or write.

Throughout Puerto Rico's colonial history, the Spanish government appointed the island's governor, who held the rank of captain general in the army. There were no courts, so the governor's rule was the law. By the early 1800s, the peninsulares and the government in Spain, fearing an uprising in Puerto Rico, used the military to keep the people under control. They **exiled** "troublemakers" or sent them to prison.

Many criollos began to see themselves as Puerto Ricans rather than Spaniards. Many of them were wealthy and well educated and believed that they had a right to govern themselves. Those who owned plantations had a hard time getting produce to markets because of the lack of roads and railroads. They wanted to decide how the money earned by their exports was spent. They wanted independence from Spain. Many Puerto Ricans also wanted the government to outlaw slavery.

MINI-BIO

RAMÓN EMETERIO BETANCES: STRIVING FOR INDEPENDENCE

Ramón Emeterio Betances (1827–1898) was born in Cabo Rojo to a wealthy family. He studied in France to become a medical doctor and also learned about democratic ideals. He returned to Puerto Rico, and when a deadly disease called cholera spread quickly through Mayagüez in 1856, he led the effort to fight it. He also helped lead the revolt at Lares in 1868. Because he worked to end slavery and win independence, the government exiled him several times. After the revolt failed, he lived in New York City and then France, where he wrote political works.

Want to know more? Visit www.factsfornow.scholastic.com and enter the keywords **Puerto Rico**.

Puerto Rico's revolution for independence from Spain began on September 23, 1868, in the small mountain city of Lares. A group of several hundred armed men and women took over Lares and proclaimed Puerto Rico an independent nation. All kinds of people were in the revolutionary movement, including landowners, doctors, lawyers, teachers, farmers, merchants, and enslaved Africans. The mastermind of the rebellion was Ramón Emeterio Betances, a doctor who was frequently exiled for his political activities.

Within 24 hours, the Spanish government crushed the revolt, which it had learned of in advance. The revolt also

WORD TO KNOW

exiled *expelled from one's own country*

failed because the revolutionaries did not have enough weapons and because Puerto Ricans who were not in the revolutionary movement did not support them.

Still, the Lares rebellion, also called the Cry of Lares, made an impact. After the rebellion, the government allowed Puerto Ricans to form political parties and vote in elections. The island was made a province of Spain, and criollos were granted Spanish citizenship. Puerto Rico could also send representatives to the parliament in Spain. In 1873, the government abolished slavery. Now everyone was paid for their labor.

Meanwhile, there was political upheaval in Spain as reformers overthrew one government after another. Between 1869 and 1873, Spain was first a **constitutional monarchy** and then a **republic**, and Puerto Ricans gained some rights. In 1873, however, Spain's king regained power. The colonial rulers in Puerto Rico again clamped down on free speech and political activists. Once again, Puerto Rico was just a colony of Spain ruled by peninsulares in San Juan.

WORDS TO KNOW

constitutional monarchy *a government with a ruler whose power is regulated by law*

republic *a government whose power belongs to the people*

THE FIRST POLITICAL PARTIES

When political parties began to form in Puerto Rico during the late 1800s, the leaders divided into two main groups: the conservative Spanish Republican Party and the progressive Liberal Reform Party. Some liberals wanted Puerto Rico to become a part of Spain, with full rights of Spanish citizenship for all Puerto Ricans. Other liberals wanted Puerto Rico to retain ties to Spain but be totally self-governing. The conservatives wanted Puerto Rico to remain under the rule of Spain's colonial officials.

Puerto Rico's economy grew worse, and the frustrations of ordinary citizens often exploded into violence. In 1897, Spain finally granted the right of self-government to Puerto Rico. Before Puerto Ricans could take advantage of their new independence, events in nearby Cuba took Puerto Rico in a surprising new direction.

MINI-BIO

LOLA RODRÍGUEZ DE TIÓ: PATRIOTIC POET

Born in San Germán, Lola Rodríguez de Tió (1843–1924) used her talent for poetry to help the cause of Puerto Rican independence. After the Lares rebellion, she wrote lyrics about the event for an existing tune, "La Borinqueña." The Spanish government exiled her, and she and her husband lived most of their lives in Cuba. In 1893, she published "Cuba y Puerto Rico Son" ("Cuba and Puerto Rico Are"), a poem that celebrates their shared heritage. She helped found the Cuban Academy of Arts and Letters in 1910 and came up with the design for Puerto Rico's flag, based on the Cuban flag.

Want to know more? Visit www.factsfornow.scholastic.com and enter the keywords **Puerto Rico**.

THE WAR OF 1898

In the late 1800s, the United States built a great navy, and its many warships played a part in the country becoming a world power. The United States wanted naval bases in the Caribbean and offered to buy Cuba from Spain, but Spain refused. At the same time, Cubans, like Puerto Ricans, wanted freedom from Spanish rule. A war of independence broke out in Cuba in 1868 and lasted 10 years. In 1878, Spain granted Cubans some political rights to end the fighting, but another struggle for independence began in 1895.

The United States warned Spain that it wanted peace in the Caribbean and told Spain to end the revolt or give up Cuba. The U.S. government sent a battleship, the USS *Maine*, to the Havana harbor to protect U.S. citizens in Cuba. On February 15, 1898, the *Maine* exploded, killing 266 of the ship's 350 officers and crewmen. To this day, the cause of the

FAQ

Q: HOW MANY PEOPLE LIVED IN PUERTO RICO WHEN THE UNITED STATES TOOK OVER?

A: Puerto Rico probably had between 660,000 and 900,000 people. According to records of the Spanish government, in 1867, Puerto Rico had a population of 656,328, including 346,437 whites and 309,891 "people of color" (blacks, mulattoes, and mestizos). According to the U.S. census in 1899, Puerto Rico had a total of 953,243 people.

The USS *Maine* exploding in the Havana harbor, February 1898

explosion remains a mystery, but at the time, U.S. newspapers and many in Congress were quick to blame Spain. With the rallying cry, "Remember the *Maine*," many demanded war with Spain, which Congress declared in April 1898.

The War of 1898 lasted only four months. Overwhelming U.S. forces crushed what remained of the Spanish army and navy. After invading Cuba, 18,000 U.S. troops moved into the southern part of Puerto Rico. Puerto Rican freedom fighters, seeking independence, provided useful information about Spain's forces to the U.S. Army.

U.S. president William McKinley demanded that Spain surrender to the United States and hand over Cuba and Puerto Rico, as well as the Philippines and Guam, Spain's island possessions in the Pacific Ocean. Spain's surrender ended the great Spanish Empire and marked the beginning of an empire for the United States.

By October 1898, the U.S. flag was flying over El Morro and all the other forts in Puerto Rico. The federal laws of the United States became the laws of Puerto Rico. Of all the former Spanish colonies in the Caribbean, only Puerto Rico had failed to win independence.

SEE IT HERE!

CASA BLANCA

After the United States took over Puerto Rico in 1898, the military commanders made the Casa Blanca, or White House, their residence. Continuously lived in since it was built in 1521, it was the oldest residence in the Americas. The descendants of Juan Ponce de León lived there for 250 years. Today, it is a museum that chronicles the history of the island.

The U.S. cruiser *St. Paul* firing on the Spanish destroyer *Terror* off San Juan, 1898

READ ABOUT

The port of San Juan, early 1900s

1917
Puerto Ricans become U.S. citizens

Cane sugar

1920s ▲
U.S. companies expand their sugar businesses in Puerto Rico

1929
Some Puerto Rican women gain the right to vote

CHAPTER FIVE

MORE MODERN TIMES

WHEN THE UNITED STATES FIRST TOOK CONTROL OF THE ISLAND, MANY PUERTO RICANS HOPED THEY WOULD BE GIVEN NEW FREEDOMS. This was not the case at first. Under a military and then a civil government controlled by the United States, Puerto Ricans saw their land become a colony of the United States as it had been a colony of Spain. The struggle for self-government soon began again.

1948
Luis Muñoz Marín becomes Puerto Rico's first elected governor

1952
Puerto Rico becomes a commonwealth

2011
Hurricane Irene strikes Puerto Rico

Members of the Harlem Hellfighters, African American and Puerto Rican soldiers in World War I

CITIZENSHIP AND WAR

In 1900, Congress returned Puerto Rico to civilian rule with a governor and an executive council appointed by the U.S. president, an elected house of representatives, courts, and a nonvoting representative to the U.S. Congress. In 1917, Congress passed the Jones-Shafroth Act, giving Puerto Ricans U.S. citizenship and individual rights. That year, the United States entered World War I, so citizenship meant that Puerto Ricans could be drafted to serve in the U.S. armed forces. Some 18,000 Puerto Ricans either enlisted or were drafted. In addition, some of Puerto Rico's 75,000 unemployed volunteered as civilian workers at military bases and defense plants.

Almost all Puerto Ricans were a blend of Spanish, African, and Indian ancestry, and unlike the United States at the time, Puerto Rico did not have a system of legal racial discrimination. But to the U.S. military, Puerto Ricans were "people of color" and were put in separate units. Many of them served in the 369th Regiment known as the Harlem Hellfighters, which included African Americans and Puerto Ricans who lived in the United States.

THE SUGAR ECONOMY

After World War I ended, U.S. companies bought land in Puerto Rico for big sugar plantations and opened new sugar mills. The U.S. government lifted taxes on sugar exported to the United States, and the production of sugar in Puerto Rico soared 1,000 percent during the 1920s. Some Puerto Ricans welcomed the opportunity to do business with the U.S. companies. Small farmers in Puerto Rico could not compete with the big corporations, however, so many sold their land. Sugar replaced almost all other crops in Puerto Rico, and about 25 percent of all Puerto Ricans worked for the U.S. sugar companies.

The sugar trade made Puerto Rico more prosperous. As a result, the government built new roads, bridges, schools, and hospitals. Puerto Ricans became better educated and healthier. But most of Puerto Rico's people continued to live in poverty. Also, Puerto Rico's economy depended almost entirely on sugar, and this proved to be disastrous.

SEE IT HERE!

THE CASTLE THAT SUGAR BUILT

Learn how sugarcane was grown and made into sugar and rum on a guided tour of the Serralles Castle on a hill above Ponce. After making a fortune in the sugar and rum business, the Serralles family built this mansion as a summer home in the 1930s. The mansion contains antique furniture, is surrounded by lovely gardens, and offers stunning views.

THE STRUGGLE FOR WOMEN'S RIGHTS

In the late 1800s and early 1900s, many Puerto Rican women worked for women's rights, especially **suffrage**. They included educator María Cadilla de Martínez, one of the first Puerto Rican women to earn a doctoral

WORD TO KNOW

suffrage *the right to vote*

MINI-BIO

FELISA RINCÓN DE GAUTIER: PIONEERING POLITICIAN

Born in Ceiba, Felisa Rincón de Gautier (1897–1994) became a champion of women's rights and one of Puerto Rico's first female political leaders. She served as the mayor of San Juan from 1946 to 1969, and she was affectionately known as Doña Felisa. As a young woman, she developed a deep concern for economically disadvantaged women. As mayor, Doña Felisa helped them by setting up day-care programs, medical centers, and legal aid. During her long life, she was awarded many honors and continued to promote causes that helped the poor.

Want to know more? Visit www.factsfornow.scholastic.com and enter the keywords **Puerto Rico**.

degree, and poets Lola Rodríguez de Tió and Julia de Burgos. When the Nineteenth Amendment was ratified in 1920, giving women on the U.S. mainland the right to vote, Puerto Rican women thought they should have the same right. However, the Nineteenth Amendment talked about the "states," and Puerto Rico was not a state. Puerto Rico's lawmakers gave women who could read and write the vote in 1929. It was not until 1935 that all women in Puerto Rico were allowed to vote. Since then, women have been elected as mayors of cities, as representatives in the legislature, and as governor.

THE GREAT DEPRESSION

In 1929, the Great Depression plunged much of the globe into an economic crisis. When sugar prices dropped all over the world, Puerto Rico slumped into poverty. Many people lost their jobs. Even during the more prosperous 1920s, Puerto Rican workers had earned an average of about $122 a year compared with about $1,500 for U.S. workers. When the Depression struck, the average Puerto Rican's annual wages fell to about $84. About 75 percent of Puerto Rico's workers were unemployed by 1934 because sugar companies cut production or completely shut down.

U.S. president Franklin D. Roosevelt set up the Puerto Rico Reconstruction Administration to help the island.

His plans, he said, "sought to secure for each citizen a place on the land which will give him a fair share in the fruits of his own labor and a position of independence and security."

Puerto Rico had been dangerously dependent on sugar. Sugarcane quickly wore out the soil and required a lot of fertilizer. In addition, hurricanes in 1928 and 1932 destroyed crops. Roosevelt called for a variety of crops to replace the island's overdependence on sugar. And he said, "Cheap and available electric power, good roads, **reforestation** and adequate housing are also essential."

The government plan helped put Puerto Ricans back to work with projects such as building roads and houses and bringing electricity to rural areas. The Great

WORD TO KNOW

reforestation *replenishing a forest by planting seeds or young trees*

First Lady Eleanor Roosevelt of the United States (in white hat) visiting Puerto Rico, 1934

Puerto Rican members of the Women's Army Auxiliary Corps assigned to service in New York City, 1945

Depression did not end, however, until World War II began in Europe in 1939. Demand for war supplies jump-started the world economy.

The United States entered the war in 1941, after Japanese planes bombed the U.S. naval fleet at Pearl Harbor, Hawai'i. Once again, Puerto Ricans answered the call, and more than 60,000 men and women served in the U.S. armed forces. Puerto Ricans of color again had to serve in units separate from whites.

Meanwhile, some Puerto Ricans had become greatly disturbed by the poverty of their people and the fact that the United States governed Puerto Rico. Members of the Puerto Rican **Nationalist** Party renewed the call for independence. They held public demonstrations and protests. In March 1937, the nationalists tried to stage a march in Ponce, but police surrounded the marchers, and gunshots rang out. No one is sure who began shooting, but in the fighting that followed, 18 marchers and two police officers were killed. The events of that day became known as the Ponce Massacre.

WORD TO KNOW

nationalist *a person who wants national independence*

OPERATION BOOTSTRAP

Puerto Rico at the end of World War II was still an agricultural country with a growing population. Better medical care had improved the people's health, so more children survived to adulthood and adults were living longer. As a result, Puerto Rico's population grew rapidly. In 1900, there were about 950,000 Puerto Ricans. By 1950, the population had more than doubled to 2 million.

Some 70,000 Puerto Rican women earned extra money for their families by doing needlework, such as sewing and embroidering garments, at home. People needed more opportunities for jobs. Puerto Rico's natural resources had been depleted in colonial times, when the Spaniards had exhausted the gold supplies. To make up for the lack of resources, the government in the mid-1900s tried to switch Puerto Rico from an agricultural economy to a manufacturing economy.

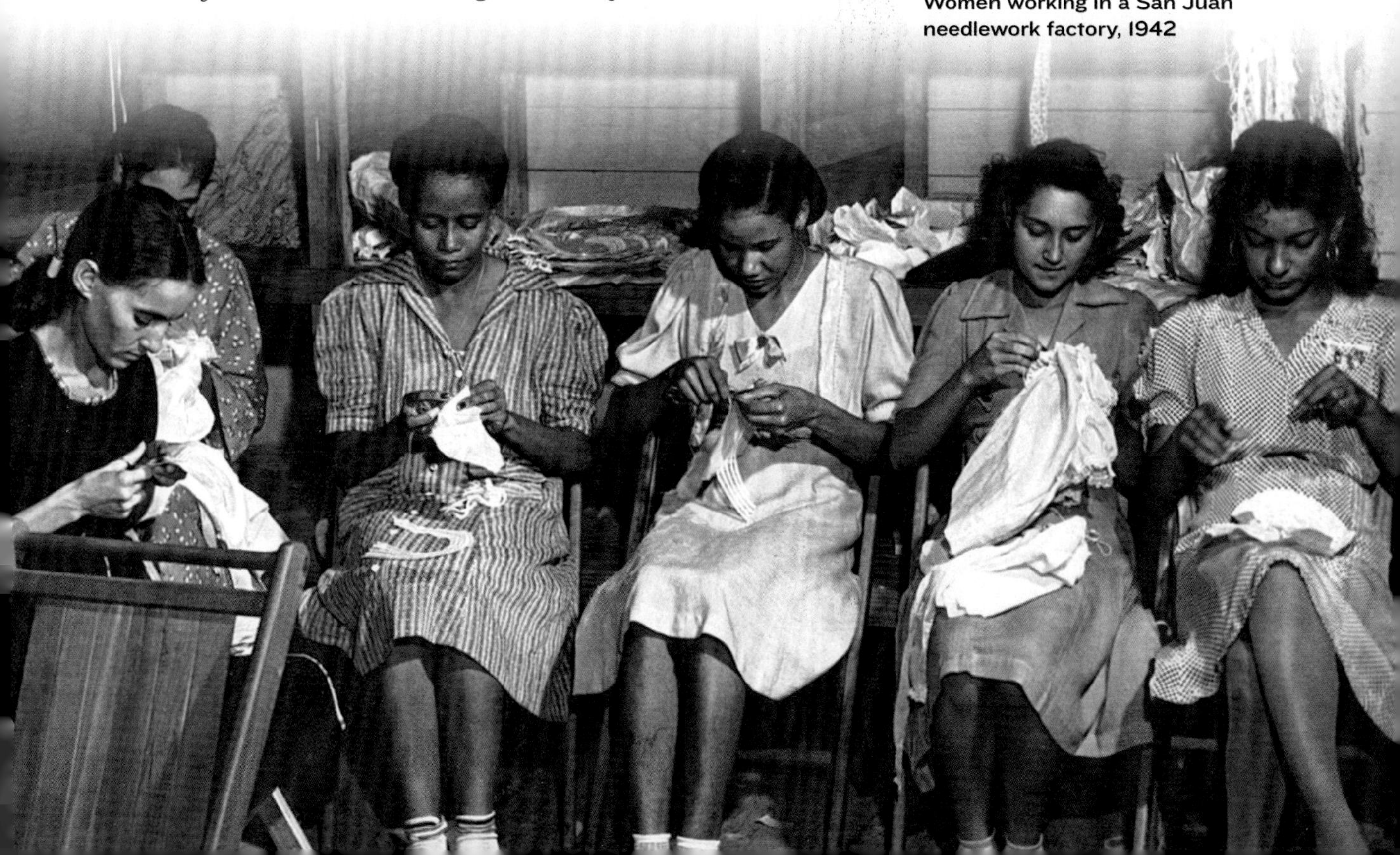

Women working in a San Juan needlework factory, 1942

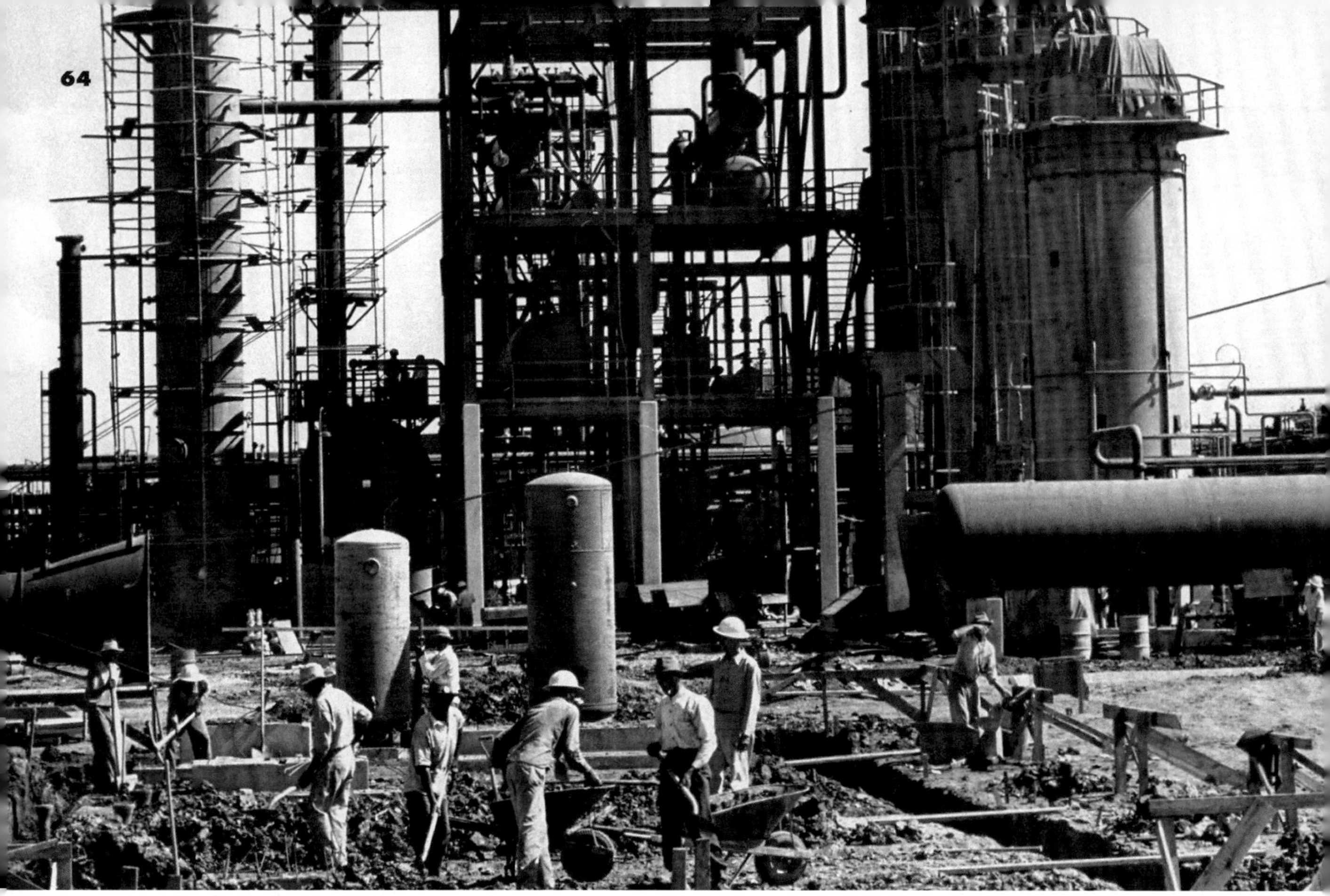

Many Puerto Rican laborers found work in oil refineries like this one.

Beginning in 1948, the Puerto Rican and U.S. governments cooperated in a program called Operation Bootstrap. It encouraged U.S. manufacturing companies to build factories in Puerto Rican cities by giving companies tax breaks and money to start up operations. Over time, the majority of Puerto Ricans left the countryside for jobs in the cities.

Unfortunately, there were still not enough jobs to go around. Because they were U.S. citizens, Puerto Ricans could move freely between Puerto Rico and the mainland. During the 1950s, some 450,000 Puerto Ricans left the island, mainly for New York City but also for Chicago, Florida, and other places on the U.S. mainland. It was the first great world migration in which people moved by airplane.

FAQ

Q8 WHAT DID THE NAME "OPERATION BOOTSTRAP" STAND FOR?

A8 A bootstrap is a loop on a boot that a person can use to pull on his or her own boots. "Bootstrap" came to mean a way for people to help themselves.

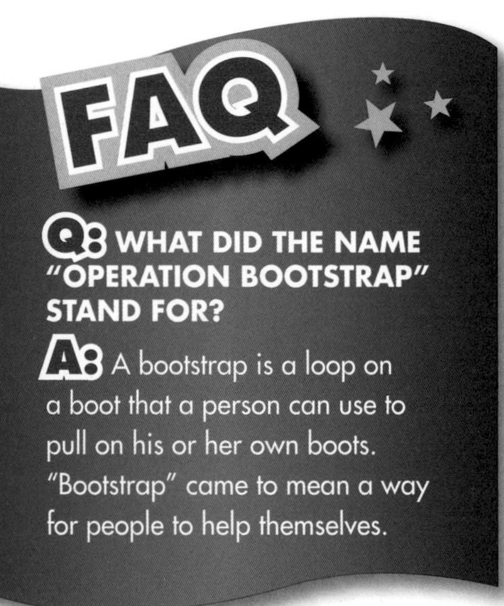

Puerto Rico: From Colony to Commonwealth

(1509–1952)

This map shows Puerto Rico when it was a Spanish colony and when it became a U.S. commonwealth.

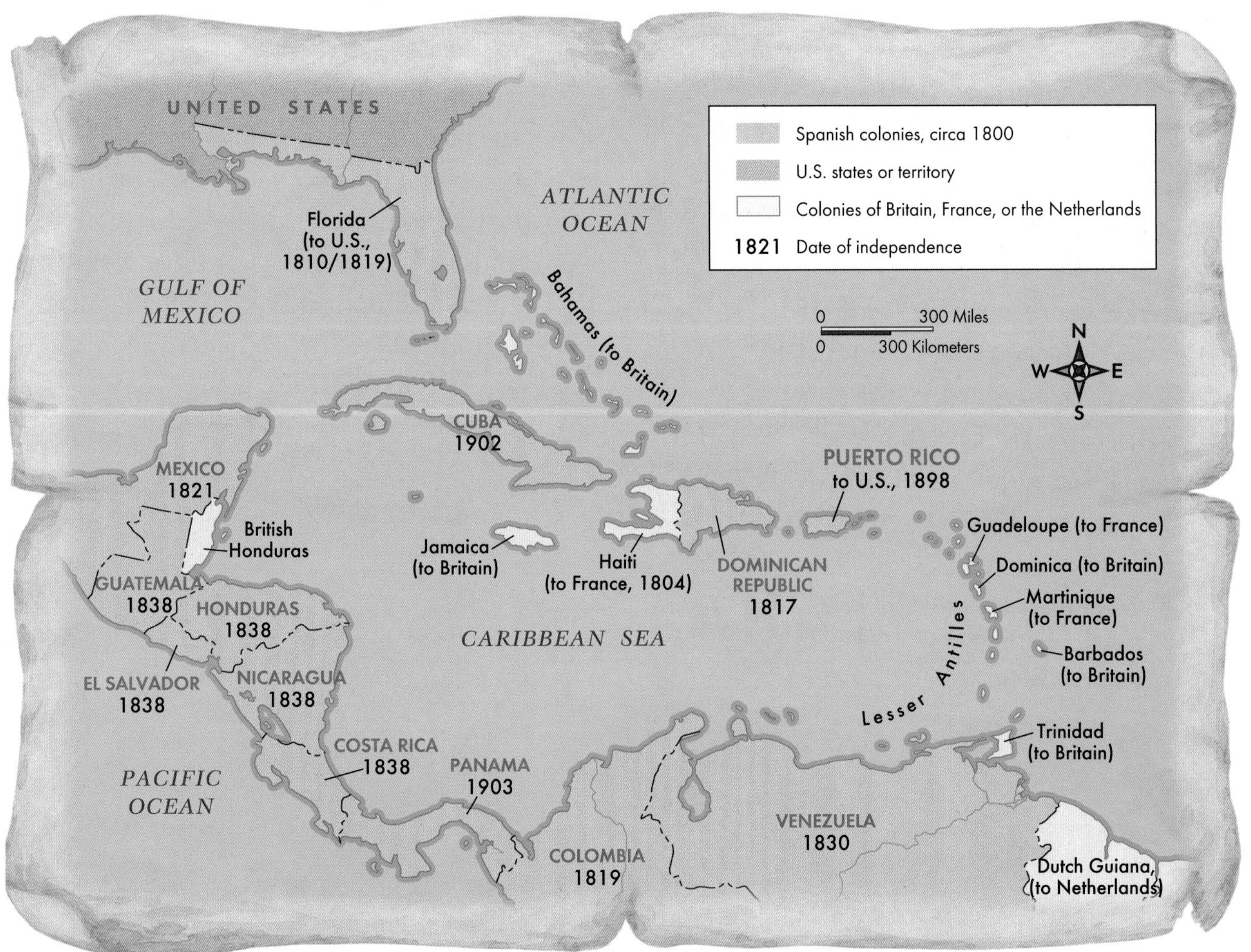

THE ROAD TO SELF-RULE

In the 1940s, the U.S. government began paving the road to Puerto Rican self-rule. In 1944, President Harry S Truman appointed the first Puerto Rican as governor, Jesús T. Piñero.

MINI-BIO

LUIS MUÑOZ MARÍN: CHAMPION OF THE COMMONWEALTH

Born in San Juan, Luis Muñoz Marín (1898–1980) was the son of a Puerto Rican publisher and statesman, and he grew up listening to political discussions. After earning a law degree and working as a writer in New York City, he returned to San Juan in 1926 to head the family newspaper. He also served in the Puerto Rican senate, founded the Popular Democratic Party, and worked to win commonwealth status for Puerto Rico. He became the first elected governor of the Commonwealth of Puerto Rico, and he was reelected three times.

Want to know more? Visit www.factsfornow.scholastic.com and enter the keywords **Puerto Rico**.

In 1948, Puerto Ricans elected their own governor, Luis Muñoz Marín. Early in his political career, Muñoz Marín believed that Puerto Rico should be an independent nation, but he came to believe that it was more important to improve the lives of Puerto Ricans. In fact, Operation Bootstrap was his idea. In 1940, he formed the Popular Democratic Party and pushed for commonwealth status, which meant Puerto Rico would be a self-governing unit

Ceremonies at El Morro to celebrate Constitution Day, 1952

of the United States. In a 1951 **referendum**, more than 80 percent of Puerto Ricans approved a commonwealth constitution. The island officially became the Commonwealth of Puerto Rico, on July 25, 1952, with Muñoz Marín as its first governor.

Not everyone was pleased, however. Nationalists wanted complete independence. In 1950, they had staged violent protests in Puerto Rico, including an attack on the governor's mansion. Also that year, they had attacked Blair House in Washington, D.C., where President Truman was staying while the White House was being repaired. Nine people were killed and about 50 others were wounded. Later, after Puerto Rico achieved commonwealth status, nationalists bitterly resented that the status was not permanent and could be changed at any time by an act of Congress. In 1954, nationalists opened fire in the U.S. House of Representatives, wounding five members of Congress.

After Alaska and Hawai'i became states in 1959, many Puerto Ricans began to think that Puerto Rico should also become a state. They formed the New Progressive Party, which promotes the idea of statehood. The pro-commonwealth and pro-statehood parties became close rivals. There have been several referendums in which Puerto Ricans voted for the status they preferred. In the first referendum in 1967, more than 60 percent supported

MINI-BIO

PEDRO ALBIZU CAMPOS: EL MAESTRO

Pedro Albizu Campos (1891–1965) was a fiery speaker in favor of an independent Puerto Rico. His eloquence earned him the nickname *El Maestro*, or "the teacher." During World War I, he interrupted his studies at Harvard University to serve in an African American unit. Albizu Campos's passionate nationalism was sometimes backed by violent actions, for which he served more than 20 years in prison. Many streets and schools in Puerto Rico and in Puerto Rican neighborhoods on the mainland are named in his honor.

Want to know more? Visit www.factsfornow.scholastic.com and enter the keywords **Puerto Rico**.

WORD TO KNOW

referendum *the people's vote on a particular issue*

MINI-BIO

SILA MARÍA CALDERÓN: PIONEERING GOVERNOR

Sila María Calderón (1942–), born in San Juan, earned a master's degree in public administration from the University of Puerto Rico, and worked in government and private industry. In 1995, she was elected mayor of San Juan. Then in 2000, as the pro-commonwealth Popular Democratic Party's candidate, she was elected Puerto Rico's first female governor. As governor, she worked to improve the economy and fight corruption.

Want to know more? Visit www.factsfornow.scholastic.com and enter the keywords **Puerto Rico**.

commonwealth status, almost 39 percent preferred statehood, and less than 1 percent wanted independence. Since then, the gap between the choice of statehood or commonwealth status has narrowed.

The issue of Puerto Rico as an independent nation again took a violent turn in 1974. A group calling itself the Fuerzas Armadas de Liberación Nacional (Armed Forces of National Liberation, or FALN) carried out more than 100 violent attacks, including bombings, in the United States to demand that Puerto Rico become a separate nation. Another group carried out violent attacks in Puerto Rico. Before being arrested, FALN members killed five people and injured more than 80 others.

THE 21ST CENTURY

In the early years of the 21st century, Puerto Ricans struggled with the continuing problems of poverty and unemployment while also debating the island's political status. Puerto Rico remains largely dependent on U.S. companies for investments and jobs, and on the federal government for aid. Roughly 41 percent of the population lives below the poverty line, and the unemployment rate of 15 percent is far more than any state on the mainland.

The government also faces economic hard times. To spur the sagging economy, some leaders think it best to continue offering **incentives** to attract business, while others think that removing government support would encourage industries to be more innovative. Attracting **biotechnology** companies is a priority for Puerto Rico.

In 2011, Puerto Ricans faced another difficult challenge. In August, Hurricane Irene slammed into the island, destroying roads and blowing down power lines. More than 1 million residents were left without power. In some places, wind speeds reached 111 miles per hour (179 kph). The high winds destroyed crops, particularly on banana and coffee plantations. Heavy rainfall caused rivers to overflow, causing wide-scale flooding. To help Puerto Rico rebuild and recover, the U.S. government granted it more than $84 million.

WORDS TO KNOW

incentives *payments or other encouragement for greater investment, for example, by businesses*

biotechnology *the use of living organisms to develop new products such as foods and medicines*

Crowds on Cristo Street in Old San Juan

READ ABOUT

A crowd celebrates at the San Sebastián Street Festival in Old San Juan.

CHAPTER SIX

PEOPLE

★

A SHOPKEEPER HURRIES ALONG THE COBBLESTONE STREETS OF OLD SAN JUAN TO OPEN HER STORE FOR BUSINESS. Tourists on a cruise ship gliding into the harbor marvel at the walls of El Morro. On a country playing field, children kick a soccer ball after school. At the Luis Muñoz Marín International Airport, a family welcomes a sister returning from New Jersey. People of Puerto Rican descent, even when they were born someplace else or are living someplace else, say they are Puerto Ricans.

LIVING IN PUERTO RICO

With some 1,088 people per square mile (418 per sq km), Puerto Rico is more densely populated than any of the 50 states, and it is one of the most densely populated islands on earth. About 94 percent of Puerto Rico's more than 3.7 million residents live in houses, condos, and apartment buildings in San Juan, Ponce, and other urban areas. The San Juan-Carolina-Bayamón metropolitan area is home to about one-third of Puerto Rico's people.

Since the mid-1900s, many Puerto Ricans have moved to the United States. By 2011, there were roughly 4.9 million people of Puerto Rican origin living on the mainland United States. Puerto Ricans are the second-largest Hispanic population in the United States, following Mexicans. New York City alone is home to an estimated

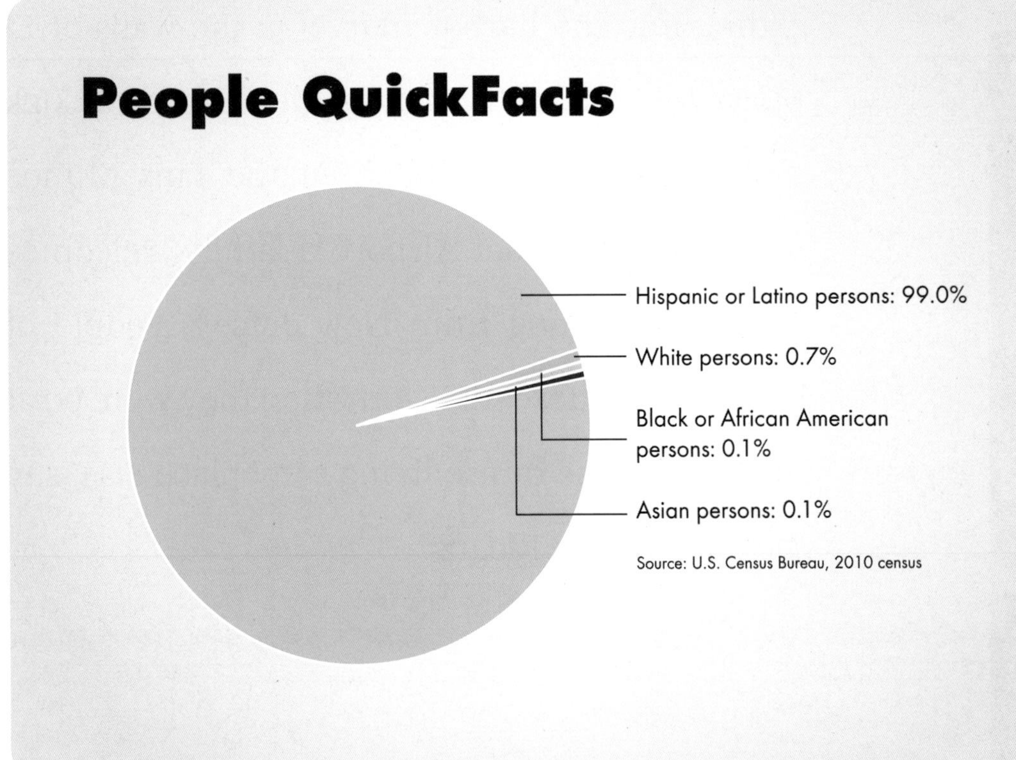

Where Puerto Ricans Live

The colors on this map indicate population density throughout the commonwealth. The darker the color, the more people live there.

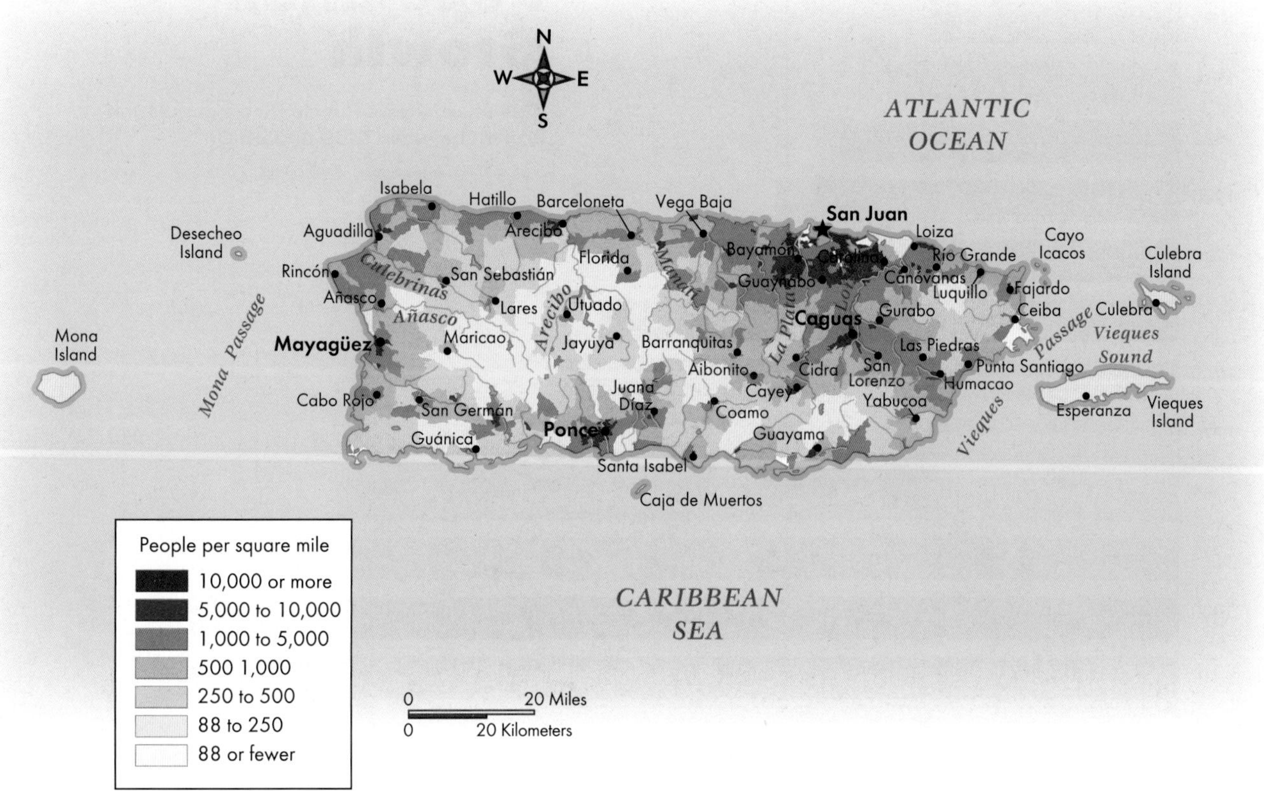

730,000 Puerto Ricans. They call themselves "Nuyorican," a combination of "New Yorker" and "Puerto Rican."

SCHOOL DAYS

Puerto Rican children must attend school from ages 6 to 17. They learn their lessons in Spanish, and English is taught as a second language. Puerto Rico's Department of Education runs the island's more than 1,500 public

Big City Life

This list shows the population of Puerto Rico's biggest cities.

City	Population
San Juan	381,931
Bayamón	185,996
Carolina	157,832
Ponce	132,502
Caguas	82,243

Source: U.S. Census Bureau, 2010 census

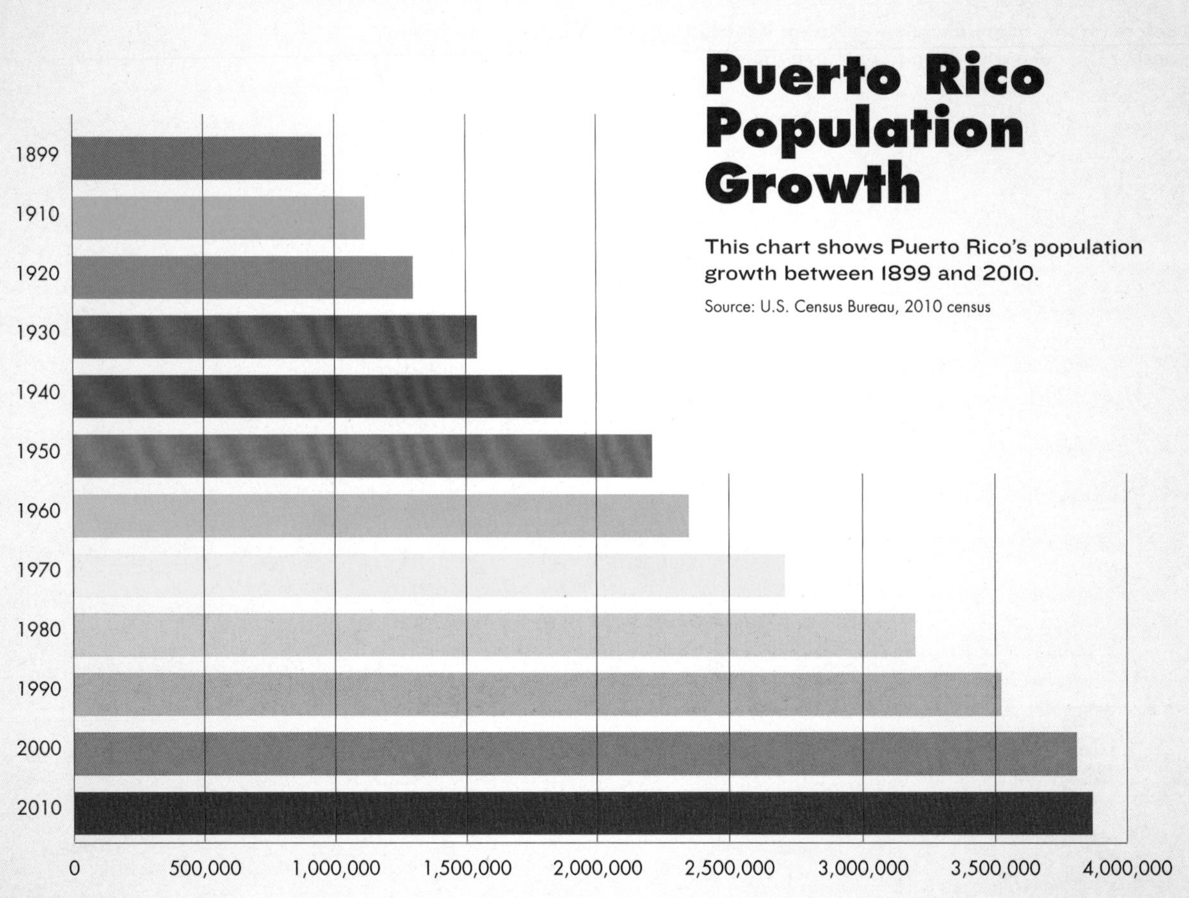

schools. More than 435,000 students from kindergarten through high school attend these schools. About 200,000 students attend the nearly 1,100 private schools in Puerto Rico. Most of these schools are operated by the Roman Catholic Church. One of Puerto Rico's most specialized schools is the Puerto Rico Baseball Academy and High School in Gurabo, which is for teenagers who want to both play Major League Baseball and have preparation for college.

Students at the University of Puerto Rico

With nearly 70 institutions of higher education, Puerto Rico has many opportunities for students who want to learn a trade or profession. The biggest and oldest university is the University of Puerto Rico, founded in 1903. The university has 11 campuses, which serve more than 64,000 students. Students earn degrees in subjects from engineering to history and study at professional schools of medicine, pharmacy, nursing, and law. Pontifical Catholic University of Puerto Rico in Ponce is noted for its school of law.

RAFAEL CORDERO: BELOVED TEACHER

Born in San Juan to black Puerto Rican parents, Rafael Cordero (1790–1868) did not have the opportunity to attend school, which was only for Puerto Rico's white upper classes. His parents could read and write, and they taught their son. When he grew up, Cordero opened an elementary school for economically disadvantaged boys. His sister, Celestina, opened a school for economically disadvantaged girls. He became such a great teacher that wealthy families sent their children to him to learn alongside the less well-off children. Many of his students grew up to be leaders in the movement to abolish slavery and in the struggle for Puerto Rican independence.

Miguel Caraballo, a mask maker from Ponce, holds one of his creations.

FOLK ARTS

The blending of African, Native, and Spanish traditions gave rise to folk arts and crafts that are uniquely Puerto Rican. Santos, small religious statues that are from 8 to 20 inches (20 to 51 cm) high, are one example. Puerto Rico's early Christians who began carving these statues may have borrowed the idea from Taínos, who carved stone or wooden statues (cemis) to honor their nature gods. Santos can be found in museums, churches, and the homes of average Puerto Ricans.

For some parades and festivals, craftspeople turn coconuts or papier-mâché into masks with horns, fangs, and bulging eyes. The style of these masks, which represent a character called Vejigante, may be the result of a blend of African and Spanish masks from the 16th century.

Puerto Rican craftspeople also make delicate lace just as lace makers did in Spain 500 years ago. The lace is used to make head coverings and to decorate clothing.

A painter in Old San Juan

FINE ARTS

Puerto Rico's first well-known painter was José Campeche (1751–1809), who produced elegant and ornate portraits and religious paintings. Francisco Oller (1833–1917) used some techniques of European impressionists in his paintings of everyday life in Puerto Rico. Impressionists were more interested in how light affects a scene than in the scene's details. In the 1900s, Ramón Frade and Miguel Pou painted figures of Puerto Rican peasants. Rafael Ferrer, a modern Puerto Rican painter and sculptor, created the painted steel sculpture *Puerto Rican Sun*, which shows the sun surrounded by two palm trees and forms an archway leading into the Bronx's Fox Park in New York City.

Musicians entertain a crowd at a festival in Old San Juan.

SALSA AND OTHER MUSICAL BLENDS

African drums, Spanish guitars, and Taíno instruments made from gourds were blended together to create the music of Puerto Rico. In the 1970s, the lively dance music called salsa was born. Music historians say that salsa came out of the Puerto Rican community in New York City after World War II as an African Caribbean blend of big band and jazz music. Ernesto "Tito" Puente, born to Puerto Rican parents in New York City, is considered the first great salsa musician. From Puerto Rico, salsa spread throughout Latin America.

CHAMPION OF BOMBA AND PLENA

As a boy growing up in San Juan and Santurce, Rafael Cepeda (1910–1996) learned about African Caribbean folk music from his parents, grandfather, and great-grandfather. He loved the sounds, rhythms, and dance movements, especially of bomba, introduced by enslaved Africans, and *plena*, a Puerto Rican form of music. In 1932, he married Caridad Brenes Caballero, a dancer, and they became a legendary bomba and plena dance team. With their children, the couple formed La Familia Cepeda, a performing group that made Puerto Rican folk music and dance even more popular.

Bomba is a form of Puerto Rican dance music that came directly from Africa and features only drums. In plena, another form of Puerto Rican dance music, the main instruments are a 10-string guitar called a *cuatro*, a tambourine, maracas, and a *guiro*. The guiro, which dates back to Taíno times, is a dried gourd with grooves on its surface that makes a raspy sound when rubbed with a stick. Puerto Rican composers in the 1800s created a gentler kind of dance music, mainly for piano, called *danza*.

MINI-BIO

LUIS MIGUEL BASTERI: POP SUPERSTAR

Singer Luis Miguel Basteri (1970–), known as Luis Miguel, has been thrilling audiences throughout the world with his exciting brand of Latin pop music for more than 30 years. Born in Santurce, he began performing professionally at 11. At age 15, he received his first Grammy Award for "I Like You Just the Way You Are," a duet with Scottish singer Sheena Easton. Since then, he has won four more Grammy Awards and four Latin Grammy Awards. Basteri is one of the world's most popular live performers, playing to sold-out audiences throughout Latin America, the United States, and Europe. In honor of his musical accomplishments, he was given a star on the Hollywood Walk of Fame in 1996.

? **Want to know more?** Visit www.factsfornow.scholastic.com and enter the keywords **Puerto Rico**.

INSPIRING WRITERS

Folktales told by jíbaros in Puerto Rico's mountains provided inspiration for several Puerto Rican writers, including Pura Belpré. In 1932, her children's book *Pérez and Martina: A Portorican Folk Tale* became the first book by a Puerto Rican writer to be published by a major U.S. publisher. *Juan Bobo: Four Folktales from Puerto Rico*, by Carmen T. Bernier-Grand, retells the adventures of a bumbling folk character.

Puerto Rico has also produced great poets and playwrights. Julia de Burgos, one of Puerto Rico's greatest poets, wrote in the 1900s. Poet and novelist Giannina Braschi wrote *Yo-Yo Boing*! (1998), the first novel in Spanglish, a kind of hybrid language that blends Spanish and English words.

FAQ

Q8 HOW ARE MARACAS MADE?

A8 The maraca, made of the round fruit of the *higuera* tree, is an instrument that came from the Taíno people. Maraca makers take the fruit out, leaving a hard shell that they fill with small pebbles. Then they attach a handle so the fruit shell can make noise when shaken.

MINI-BIO

JOSÉ FERRER: STAGE AND SCREEN LEGEND

Born in Santurce, José Ferrer (1912–1992) launched his legendary acting career in 1935. He quickly became known as one of the top performers on Broadway, winning Tony Awards for both acting and directing. Ferrer's success on the stage led to a successful Hollywood career as well. In 1950, he won an Academy Award for his performance as the title character in *Cyrano de Bergerac*. For the next several decades, he continued to play memorable roles in a wide variety of films and plays. In 1985, he became the first actor ever to be awarded the National Medal of Arts.

Want to know more? Visit www.factsfornow.scholastic.com and enter the keywords **Puerto Rico**.

Another great Puerto Rican writer, René Marqués, wrote a play called *The Oxcart*, about the mass migration of Puerto Ricans to New York City in the 1950s. Poet Miguel Algarín was born in Puerto Rico and moved to New York as a child. In the 1970s, he helped found the Nuyorican Poets Café on New York City's Lower East Side. Today, the café offers poetry readings and hosts theatrical and musical performances.

A player steals second base during the annual Puerto Rican All-Star baseball game.

BIRTHPLACE OF BASEBALL PLAYERS

Since the first nine-inning game was played in Puerto Rico in 1898, Puerto Ricans have been in love with baseball. Puerto Rico does not have its own Major League Baseball team, but it has supplied U.S. teams with more than 200 outstanding players, including Roberto Clemente, Félix Millán, Orlando Cepeda, José Cruz, and Ivan Rodriguez. Many Major League players got their start in the Puerto Rican Professional Baseball League.

Soccer, volleyball, and beach volleyball are also popular sports in Puerto Rico.

MINI-BIO

ROBERTO CLEMENTE: BASEBALL LEGEND

Carolina-born Roberto Clemente (1934–1972) played 18 seasons in Major League Baseball for the Pittsburgh Pirates, from 1955 to 1972. He was named the National League's Most Valuable Player in 1966. He won 12 Gold Glove Awards and led the league in scoring during four different seasons. Clemente died in a plane crash while attempting to deliver aid to earthquake victims in Nicaragua, one of his many charitable efforts for Latin countries. In 1973, he became the first Puerto Rican player inducted into the Baseball Hall of Fame.

Want to know more? Visit www.factsfornow.scholastic.com and enter the keywords **Puerto Rico**.

PUERTO RICAN NAMES

Following the Spanish tradition, Puerto Ricans often use two last names. The first last name is the father's surname, and the second last name is the mother's surname. For example, Luis Muñoz Marín was the son of Luis Muñoz Rivera and Amalia Marín Castilla. Puerto Ricans sometimes use both surnames, and sometimes they use only their father's surname. Names are alphabetized by the first of the two surnames.

WOW

Puerto Rico is an independent nation as far as the Olympic Games are concerned and therefore sends its own team. In the competitions, however, each athlete on the team can choose whether he or she wants to represent Puerto Rico or the United States.

HOW TO TALK LIKE A PUERTO RICAN

Puerto Ricans call their island Borinquen or Borikén, the name that Taínos used for the island before the Spanish arrived. Puerto Ricans call themselves Boricuas.

Puerto Rico has two official languages, Spanish and English. At home, Boricuas speak Spanish. Just as American English is different from British English, so Puerto Rican Spanish is different from the language in Spain. Over time, Puerto Rican Spanish evolved to include words from not only the Taíno people but also the island's various immigrant groups.

The biggest outside influence on Puerto Rican Spanish today is English. For example, *parquear el carro* means "to park the car," *flash* means "camera," and *la Internet* means "the Internet." Puerto Ricans who speak English, especially on the U.S. mainland, sometimes mix so much English into their Spanish that they end up speaking Spanglish.

Okra

HOW TO EAT LIKE A PUERTO RICAN

Like everything else in Puerto Rico, the food is a blend of Taíno, Spanish, and African ingredients. Taínos feasted on seafood and tropical fruits. Spaniards added pork, beef, and rice. Africans brought plantains, bananas, okra, yams, and pigeon peas, a light tan pea with a nutty flavor. Puerto Ricans flavor their main dishes with spice mixtures called *adobo*—which includes peppercorns, oregano, garlic, salt, olive oil, and lime juice—and *sofrito*—which includes onions, garlic, coriander, peppers, and annatto seeds. Puerto Ricans call the dishes made from these blends *cocina criolla*, which means "Creole cooking."

Plantain

MENU

WHAT'S ON THE MENU IN PUERTO RICO?

Flan

Arroz con Pollo (Rice with Chicken)

Arroz con pollo is a popular dish in many parts of Latin America. In Puerto Rico, the dish combines white rice and pieces of chicken with tomato paste and vegetables such as bell peppers, olives, and peas. Some cooks add ham.

Tostones (Puerto Rican Fried Plantains)

Tostones are slices of fried plantain, a starchy version of a banana. You can top your tostones with *mojo*, a sauce made from olive oil, garlic, and lemon or lime juice.

Arroz con Gandules (Rice with Pigeon Peas)

To make this traditional dish, add boiled pigeon peas to a mixture of ham or salt pork, garlic, peppers, onions, tomatoes, and sofrito. Spoon the mixture over cooked white rice.

Lechon Asado (Roasted Pig)

Often served at big parties, this recipe calls for one whole pig seasoned with garlic, lemons, cilantro, and other herbs and spices. Traditionally, the whole pig is cooked on a spit over a fire.

Fresh Fruit

Plenty of tropical fruits, such as bananas, papayas, passion fruit, and mangoes, grow in Puerto Rico.

Papayas

TRY THIS RECIPE
Flan

Most Spanish-speaking cultures enjoy some version of this treat. Here is a recipe from Puerto Rico. Keep a grown-up nearby to help.

Ingredients:

1½ cups sugar
2 tablespoons water
1 12-ounce can evaporated milk
1 14-ounce can condensed milk
5 eggs
1 teaspoon vanilla
A pinch of salt

Instructions:

1. Preheat the oven to 350°F.
2. In a nonstick pan, combine 1 cup of the sugar and the water. Cook over low heat until all the sugar melts. As it melts, it will darken into a light brown caramel syrup. (Be careful not to let it get any darker than this!) Pour the syrup into an 8-inch pie pan or baking dish and quickly swirl it around to cover the bottom and sides. Set aside to cool.
3. In a bowl, whisk together all the other ingredients, including the remaining ½ cup of sugar. Pour the mixture through a strainer over the caramel in the baking dish.
4. Put the baking dish inside a larger pan, then put that in the oven. Carefully pour boiling water into the larger pan, to about ½ inch from the top of the baking dish. Bake for 1 hour, or until a knife inserted into the center of the flan comes out clean.
5. After the flan has cooled, lay a plate upside down over the baking dish. Carefully flip it over so the custard slides out. Enjoy!

READ ABOUT

The Puerto Rico Senate debates a bill in 2013.

GOVERNMENT

★

PUERTO RICANS DO NOT PAY TAXES TO THE U.S. GOVERNMENT AND CANNOT VOTE TO ELECT A U.S. PRESIDENT. Puerto Ricans elect a representative to the U.S. Congress, but the representative has no vote.

Is Puerto Rico's special status a good thing or a bad thing? Everyone, from kids in school to parents at home, debates it. Should Puerto Rico become a state, an independent nation, or stay the way it is? To understand this debate, it helps to know how the government of Puerto Rico operates.

MINI-BIO

LUIS MUÑOZ RIVERA: CHAMPION OF U.S. CITIZENSHIP

Luis Muñoz Rivera (1859–1916), born in Barranquitas when Spain ruled Puerto Rico, used a newspaper that he founded to win support for independence. After the United States took control of Puerto Rico, he worked toward self-government. As resident commissioner from 1910 until his death, he championed U.S. citizenship for all Puerto Ricans. His son, Luis Muñoz Marín, became Puerto Rico's first elected governor.

Want to know more? Visit www.factsfornow.scholastic.com and enter the keywords **Puerto Rico**.

THE CONSTITUTION

Between 1898 and 1952, Puerto Rico was governed by the United States. After a series of steps toward self-rule in the 1940s, Puerto Ricans in 1952 voted to adopt a constitution making the island a commonwealth of the United States. The constitution makes Puerto Rico a self-governing unit voluntarily tied to the United States.

Like the constitutions of the states and the nation, the constitution of the Commonwealth of

El Capitolio in San Juan

Capital City

This map shows places of interest in San Juan, Puerto Rico's capital city.

Puerto Rico calls for three separate branches of government. The legislative branch makes the commonwealth's laws, the executive branch carries out the laws and makes sure the government runs smoothly, and the judicial branch ensures that the laws are applied justly to all.

San Juan is home to the commonwealth's government. The capitol building, El Capitolio, houses the legislative branch. Completed in 1929, it is one of the newer official buildings in San Juan. Its dome was not completed until 1961. El Capitolio is located in the area called Old San Juan, which is a walled city on the small harbor island where the Spanish settled.

The heart of the executive branch is the governor's mansion, La Fortaleza, an old fort dating from the 1500s.

Capitol Facts

Here are some fascinating facts about Puerto Rico's commonwealth capitol.

Area of building: 51,814 square feet (4,814 sq m)
Number of levels: 3
Height of building: 147 feet (45 m)
Exterior construction materials: Concrete and steel with marble facing
Date of completion, main building: 1929
Date of completion, dome: 1961

SEE IT HERE!

LA FORTALEZA

The home of Puerto Rico's governors, La Fortaleza is surrounded by beautiful gardens and 16th-century cannons. The cannons are a reminder that La Fortaleza was built as a fort between 1533 and 1540, with two stone towers and massive stone walls. Since 1640, La Fortaleza has been the residence of the island's Spanish governor, making it the oldest governor's mansion in the Western Hemisphere. In 1846, La Fortaleza was remodeled to make it less like a fort and more like a home.

Today, it houses the office and residence of Puerto Rico's chief executive.

The Puerto Rico Supreme Court meets in its own modern, three-story concrete and glass building in San Juan's Luis Muñoz Rivera Park. The light, airy building was completed in 1956.

THE LEGISLATIVE BRANCH

The Legislative Assembly decides how to spend tax money, can amend the constitution, and passes internal measures that do not conflict with U.S. laws. Federal laws apply in Puerto Rico as they do in the United States.

The Legislative Assembly is made up of two houses, the senate and the house of representatives. There must be at least 27 senators and 51 representatives, but there can be more. If any political party wins more than a two-thirds majority of either the House or the Senate, additional at-large members can be granted to the opposing party. No party can have more than two-thirds of the seats in either house.

Members of both the senate and the house are elected to serve four-year terms. Two senators are elected from each of Puerto Rico's eight senatorial districts, and one representative comes from each of the 40 representative districts. In addition, all Puerto Ricans vote to elect 11 senators and 11 representatives at-large, which means they do not represent any district.

Representing Puerto Ricans

This list shows the number of elected officials who represent Puerto Rico, both on the commonwealth and national levels.

OFFICE	NUMBER	LENGTH OF TERM
Commonwealth senators	at least 27	4 years
Commonwealth representatives	at least 51	4 years
U.S. senators	0	—
U.S. representatives	1 (nonvoting)	4 years
Presidential electors	0	—

THE EXECUTIVE BRANCH

Puerto Rico's governor is the head of the executive branch. Voters elect the governor to serve a four-year term, and there

Governor Alejandro García Padilla speaks at his inauguration ceremony in 2013.

is no limit to how many terms a governor may serve. The governor appoints the heads of departments in the executive branch, such as justice, state, education, and agriculture. The head of each department is called a secretary. The governor also appoints all judges, including the Puerto Rico Supreme Court justices, and the heads of public corporations owned by the commonwealth, such as those providing electricity, water, and transportation. The senate must confirm the appointments.

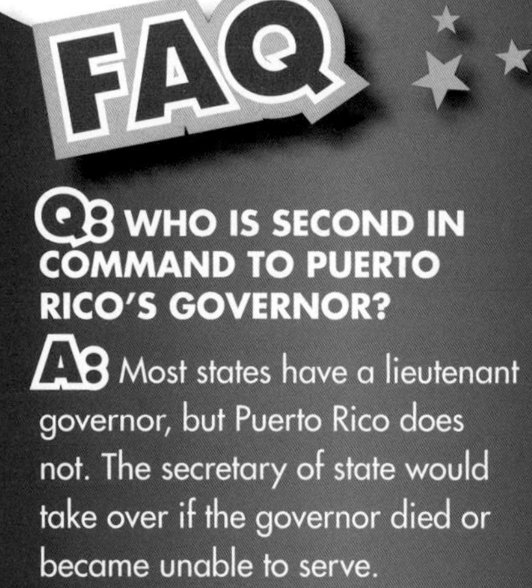

Q: WHO IS SECOND IN COMMAND TO PUERTO RICO'S GOVERNOR?

A: Most states have a lieutenant governor, but Puerto Rico does not. The secretary of state would take over if the governor died or became unable to serve.

A police officer patrols the streets of Old San Juan.

THE JUDICIAL BRANCH

Puerto Rico's judicial branch includes the courts and the judges who serve on them. The judicial branch makes sure Puerto Rico's laws do not violate the constitution. Local cases are heard in the municipal and district courts. The next judicial level is the superior court. When a decision in a court is challenged, it goes to the circuit court of appeals. Puerto Rico's highest court is the supreme court. Its head judge is called the chief justice. Six other judges serve on the supreme court.

A federal district court deals with U.S. laws. The U.S. president names judges to this court. Someone who does not like a federal court decision may appeal to the U.S. Supreme Court.

Puerto Rico Government

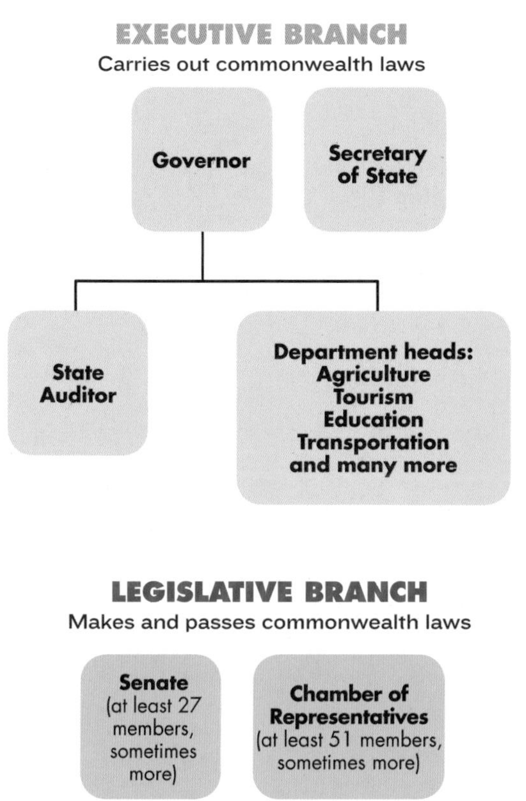

JUDICIAL BRANCH
Enforces commonwealth laws

Supreme Court
Court of Appeals
Superior Court
District Courts
Municipal Courts

LOCAL GOVERNMENT

Puerto Rico is divided into 78 municipalities, each of which is centered in a city, town, or village. An elected mayor and municipal assembly govern each municipality, and the mayor names an auditor and treasurer for each one. A municipality is further divided into neighborhoods, and each neighborhood is divided into sectors.

PUERTO RICO AND THE UNITED STATES

Puerto Rico's government takes care of the island's internal issues, such as education and transportation, and collects taxes to pay for these services. The U.S. federal

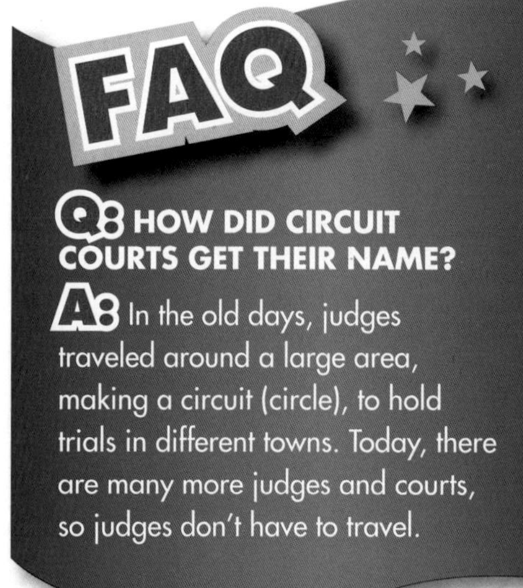

Puerto Rico Municipalities

This map shows the 78 municipalities in Puerto Rico. San Juan, the commonwealth capital, is indicated with a star.

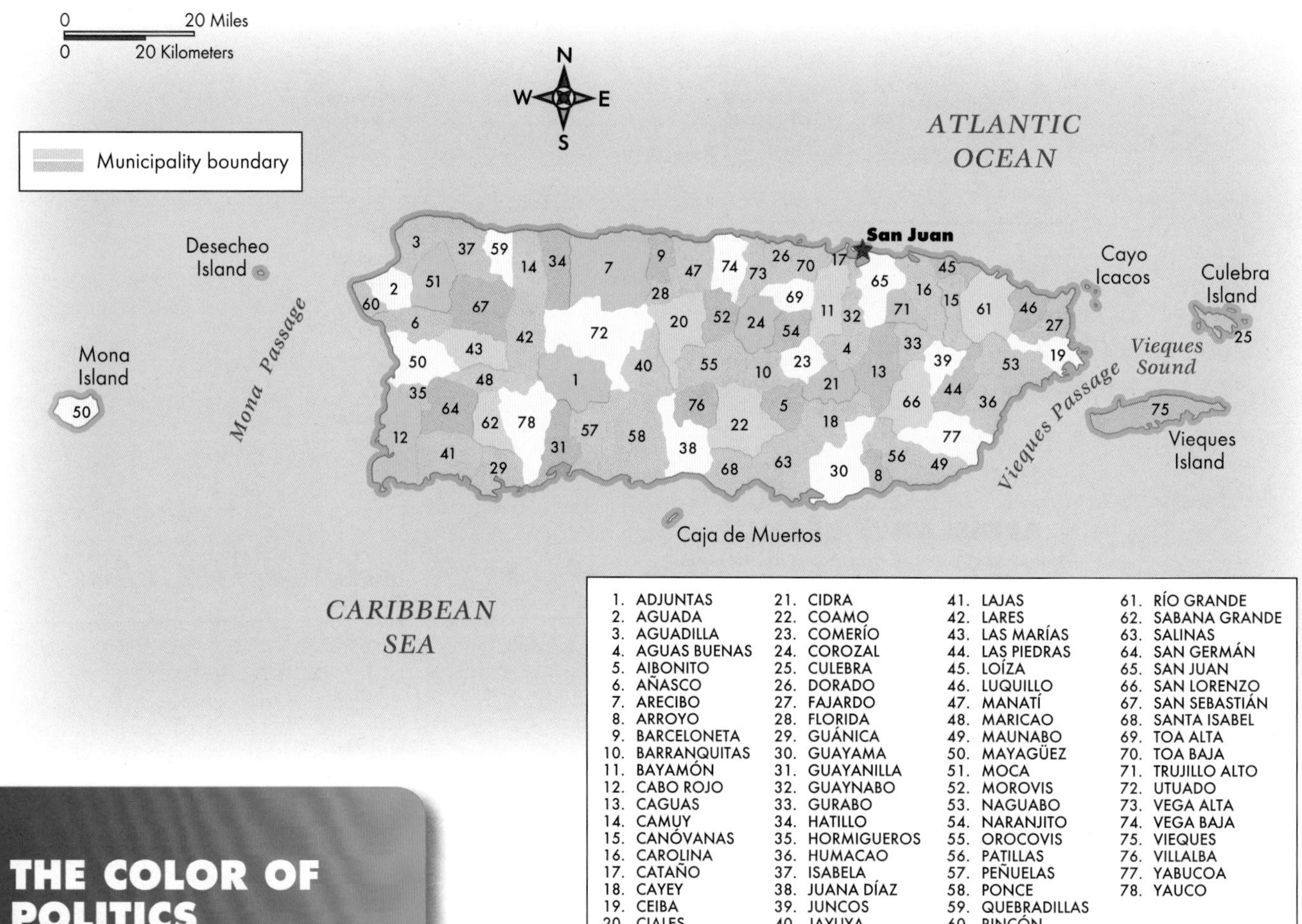

THE COLOR OF POLITICS

Puerto Rico's three major political parties are known by their colors. Blue is the color of the New Progressive Party, which favors statehood for Puerto Rico. Red is the color of the Popular Democratic Party, which wants Puerto Rico to remain a commonwealth. Green is the color of the Puerto Rican Independence Party, which wants Puerto Rico to become a separate nation.

government is responsible for the island's defense, immigration policies, military bases, money, and all other areas that are handled by the federal government in the states.

All Puerto Ricans are U.S. citizens and can travel freely to any place in the United States. Some Puerto Ricans are happy with their relationship with the United States. Others want Puerto Rico to become a state, and still others believe that Puerto Rico should be an independent nation. Most Puerto Ricans, however, want any future relationship to be one that will allow them to always be citizens of the United States.

THINK ABOUT IT!

Puerto Rico's Status

Puerto Ricans have been debating the political status of their island for decades: should it become an independent nation, become a state, or stay a commonwealth?

The Puerto Rican Independence Party wants Puerto Rico to become a country. "Independence. To us independence is synonymous with the development of a democracy, the full protection of civil and political rights, and a decent way of life based on a work ethic," argues Rubén Berríos Martínez, president of the Puerto Rican Independence Party. "Independence will provide the means and conditions to develop a more permanent, more just, and more self-reliant economic growth."

Members of the New Progressive Party want Puerto Rico to become the 51st state in the United States. They point out that while Puerto Rico is part of the United States, Puerto Ricans cannot vote for the president, do not have voting representatives in Congress, and do not get their fair share of federal programs and funds. "Puerto Rico's status is the principal reason why the territory [Puerto Rico] has confronted severe economic challenges for decades and why thousands of our best and brightest residents relocate to the states every month in search of better opportunities," says Pedro R. Pierluisi, president of the New Progressive Party. "We seek the same rights and responsibilities as our fellow citizens in the 50 states. Nothing more and nothing less."

The Popular Democratic Party (PDP) wants to keep the existing commonwealth status, which gives Puerto Ricans U.S. citizenship while allowing them to be self-governing. "I do not believe in statehood," says PDP president Alejandro García Padilla. "That would be disastrous for the economy of Puerto Rico. It would turn Puerto Rico into a ghetto, an entire country turned into a Latin American ghetto. And we cannot allow that to happen. I don't believe in independence."

Q8 DOES PUERTO RICO ELECT REPRESENTATIVES TO CONGRESS?

A8 Puerto Ricans elect one representative to Congress, the resident commissioner to the U.S. House of Representatives. The resident commissioner serves on congressional committees and votes on measures considered by a committee, but the commissioner cannot vote when a bill goes before the full House.

Commonwealth Flag

The Puerto Rican flag has five red and white stripes. The three red stripes symbolize the blood that feeds the three branches of government. The two white stripes remind citizens of their rights and the freedom of the individual. On the left of the flag is a single white five-pointed star inside a blue triangle. The star stands for the Commonwealth of Puerto Rico, and the triangle represents the three branches of its republican government. The flag was designed around 1895 in New York City by Puerto Rican and Cuban political exiles who were fighting together to win independence of the two islands from Spain. As a result, Cuba's flag has the same design with the blue and red areas reversed. Puerto Rico's flag was officially adopted in 1952.

Commonwealth Seal

Puerto Rico's seal is based on its 16th-century coat of arms. The green background represents the island's fertility. The lamb is sitting on one of the books in the Christian Bible, which represents Catholic Spain. The *F* and the quiver of arrows represent King Ferdinand. The *I* and the yoke represent Queen Isabella. The Latin motto "*Joannes Est Nomen Ejus*" means "John Is Its Name." This refers to the first Spanish name for Puerto Rico, which was San Juan, or Saint John. The images in the border represent different parts of medieval Spain: castles for Castile, lions for León, flags for Aragon and Sicily, and crosses for Jerusalem.

READ ABOUT

Workers on a construction site in San Juan

ECONOMY

★

DID YOU EVER WAKE UP WITH A STUFFY NOSE? Maybe you took some cold medicine before heading off to school. That medicine might have come from a company in Puerto Rico. You won't see "Made in Puerto Rico" on the bottle, however, because Puerto Rico is part of the United States. That medicine was made in the USA.

Copper blocks are manufactured at this Puerto Rico factory.

THE TIES THAT BIND

Throughout its recorded history, Puerto Rico's economy has been tied to the policies of another government. From the 1500s to the late 1800s, Spain controlled Puerto Rico's economy and used Puerto Rico as a military base. Since 1898, when the United States took control, Puerto Rico's economy has been very closely tied to the United States and U.S. policies regarding the island.

In the 1940s, Operation Bootstrap, a program run by Puerto Rico's government with U.S. cooperation, encouraged factories to open. The U.S. government helped out by offering companies tax breaks and money to start up factories. In addition, Puerto Rico could send manufactured products to the United States **duty-free**. As a

WORD TO KNOW

duty-free *without having to pay tax on exports or imports*

Top Products

Agriculture	Sugarcane, coffee, pineapples, plantains, bananas, livestock, chickens
Manufacturing	Medicines, electronics, clothing, food products, medical equipment
Other	Government, retail trade, tourism

result, manufacturing grew rapidly in Puerto Rico and passed agriculture in importance to the economy in the 1950s and 1960s.

Companies send raw materials for making goods to Puerto Rico, and Puerto Rican companies export finished products to the United States and other countries. At first, manufacturing companies made items such as clothing, wood products, and ceramics. But high-tech companies soon realized that because of government incentives, building factories in Puerto Rico was good business. Drug companies, computer manufacturers, and makers of other electronic products are now the leading manufacturers. They have also become Puerto Rico's leading employers.

MANUFACTURING

Puerto Rico has a total labor force of about 950,000. About 84,000 Puerto Ricans work in manufacturing. Pharmaceuticals, or medicines, are by far the most important manufacturing business in Puerto Rico. Many of the biggest drug companies in the world have factories for making medicines in Puerto Rico's rural communities, as well as in San Juan, Ponce, and other cities. In fact, Puerto Rico is the fifth-largest drug-making location in the world. Roughly 20,000 Puerto Ricans work for drug companies, with about another 90,000 people employed in related jobs.

DEIRDRE P. CONNELLY: MAKING MEDICINES

Deirdre P. Connelly (1960–), born in San Juan, has devoted her professional life to a career with giant drug maker Eli Lilly and Company. She worked her way up from a starting position as sales representative in 1983 to several major executive posts. In 1995, she became general manager of Lilly's operations in Puerto Rico, and in 2005 became the president of Lilly USA. In 2009, she became the president of North American operations for the English pharmaceutical giant GlaxoSmithKline.

Want to know more? Visit www.factsfornow.scholastic.com and enter the keywords **Puerto Rico**.

Other Puerto Ricans produce parts and programs for computers. Electronic devices, such as pacemakers and other medical equipment, are also important to the island's manufacturing economy.

Major Agricultural and Mining Products

This map shows where Puerto Rico's major agricultural and mining products come from. See a sugarcane stalk? That means sugarcane is found there.

SERVICE INDUSTRIES

Who issues your driver's license or sets up a Social Security account so that you can get a job? Government workers handle these tasks and do all kinds of other jobs that keep the government running. In Puerto Rico, about 274,000 workers hold government jobs.

Retail trade is another important part of Puerto Rico's service industry. In addition to supply-

Workers at this café are part of Puerto Rico's service industry.

KIMBERLY CASIANO: A LEADER IN BUSINESS

Kimberly Casiano (1957–) was born in New York City but moved with her family to Puerto Rico when she was 12 years old. After earning degrees from Princeton and Harvard universities, she ran her own business and then became president of the family business, Casiano Communications, Puerto Rico's largest Hispanic periodical publishing company. In addition, in 2003 she was elected to Ford Motor Company's board of directors, becoming the first Hispanic woman ever to serve on the board of a top U.S. corporation.

Want to know more? Visit www.factsfornow.scholastic.com and enter the keywords **Puerto Rico**.

ing goods for Puerto Rican shoppers, retail stores serve the 3 million tourists who flock to the island every year. Tourists bring in more than $3 billion a year, making tourism an important part of Puerto Rico's service economy. In fact, in the early 2000s, it was the fastest-growing part of the island's economy.

In an average year, Puerto Rico's coffee plantations produce about 14,000 to 15,000 tons of coffee.

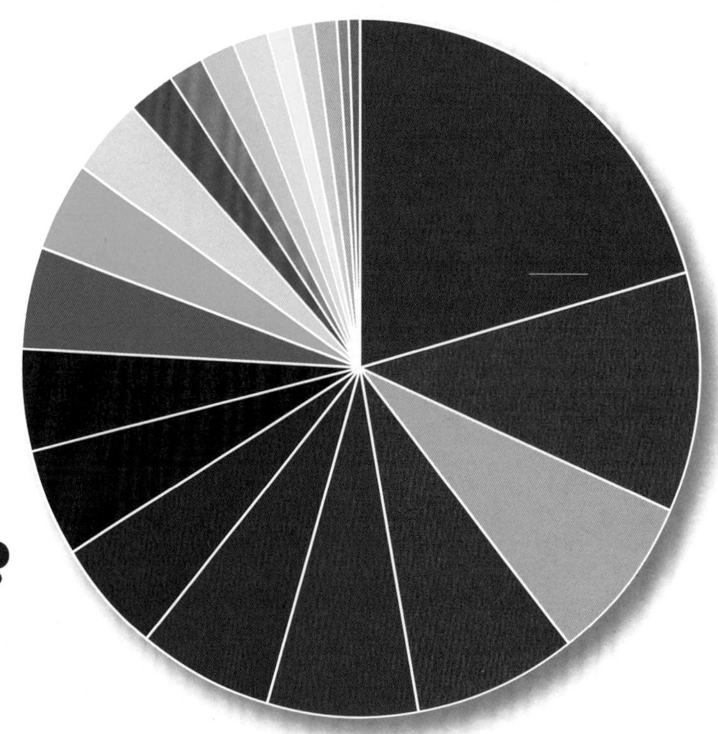

What Do Puerto Ricans Do?

This color-coded chart shows what industries Puerto Ricans work in.

Percent	Occupation
18.8%	Office and administrative support 178,450
10.1%	Sales and related occupations 101,910
7.2%	Production 68,700
7.0%	Food preparation and serving related 66,730
6.6%	Protective service 62,320
5.8%	Transportation and material moving 55,050
4.8%	Healthcare practitioner and technical 45,600
4.7%	Buildings and grounds cleaning and maintenance 44,760
4.4%	Business and financial operations 41,980
4.2%	Construction and extraction 39,500
3.8%	Management 36,110
3.3%	Installation, maintenance, and repair 31,120
2.0%	Community and social services 18,730
1.5%	Healthcare support 13,980
1.3%	Architecture and engineering 12,150
1.2%	Personal care and service 11,840
1.0%	Computer and mathematical 9,360
0.8%	Life, physical, and social science 7,160
0.7%	Arts, design, entertainment sports 6,590
0.5%	Legal 4,640
0.1%	Farming, fishing, and forestry 1,340

Source: U.S. Census Bureau, 2010 census

A farmworker on a banana plantation in Maricao

More than 1 million visitors arrive each year on cruise ships alone to shop, visit museums and art galleries, and take tours of Puerto Rico's historic places. Other tourists fly in to stay at hotels and beach resorts all over the island. Puerto Rico's tourism industry supplies about 62,000 jobs at hotels, restaurants, tour companies, and other businesses that serve the visitors.

PRODUCTS FROM THE LAND

In 2010, Puerto Rico had about 10,400 farms with sales of $1,000 or more, according to the U.S. Department of Agriculture. Most farms are small, with an average of about 43 acres (17 ha). The main crops are sugarcane, coffee, pineapples, bananas, plantains, peas, beans, and sweet potatoes.

Puerto Rico has little in the way of mineral resources. The main minerals produced are cement, crushed stone, sand, and gravel.

Even though Puerto Rico is surrounded by ocean, the island's commercial fishing industry remains small. Sport fishing, however, brings a number of tourists to the island.

CHALLENGES

Puerto Rico has long suffered from high unemployment, despite government efforts to attract industry and create jobs. The problem grew more serious after 1996, when the U.S. government changed the rules governing tax incentives to manufacturing companies. By the end of 2007, five drug companies had closed down plants in Puerto Rico or were planning to do so. The closings cost 3,000 Puerto Ricans their jobs.

In 2005, only about 40 percent of people ages 16 to 65 were employed, compared with almost 70 percent of that age group on the mainland United States. Puerto Rico's unemployment rate during the early 2000s hovered between 11 and 12 percent.

Government assistance has helped Puerto Ricans survive. Government support to Puerto Ricans totals about $11 billion a year and includes welfare and retirement payments, food stamps, and Medicare. Puerto Rico's commonwealth government, however, fell deep into debt. In 2006, threatened with a government shutdown, Puerto Rico's Legislative Assembly passed the island's first sales tax, a 5.5 percent tax.

High energy costs in the early 2000s drove up Puerto Rico's cost of living and have been a factor in slowing economic growth. Some people think that Puerto Rico is too dependent on government assistance. Some believe that the solution to creating jobs lies in reducing government regulations.

Tourism is an important part of Puerto Rico's economy, and these cruise ships in San Juan are part of that industry.

Other economists believe that finding solutions to Puerto Rico's economic problems will not be easy and will require the cooperation of business, industry, government, and the Puerto Rican people. "All sectors of the economic landscape [need to] contribute ideas, strategies, and approaches to solve this puzzle," said Manuel E. Maldonado, of Quality for Business Services, a company that helped prepare an analysis of Puerto Rico's economy. "I am confident Puerto Rico can stand up with pride, resolve, and strength of will to decisively deal with the current reality."

ATLANTIC
OCEAN

CARIBBEAN
SEA

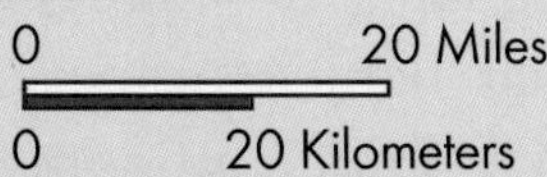

CHAPTER NINE

TRAVEL GUIDE

TRAVEL GUIDE

★

RELAX ON A BEAUTIFUL BEACH, HIKE THROUGH A TROPICAL RAIN FOREST, OR LOOK OUT OF A STONE SENTRY BOX AND IMAGINE THE SAILS OF A PIRATE SHIP APPEARING ON THE HORIZON. Puerto Rico has wonderful natural areas, plus museums and historic sites that will take you through thousands of years of Caribbean civilization. There's a lot to do, so let's get going!

← Follow along with this travel map. We'll begin in the San Juan area and travel all the way to Rincón!

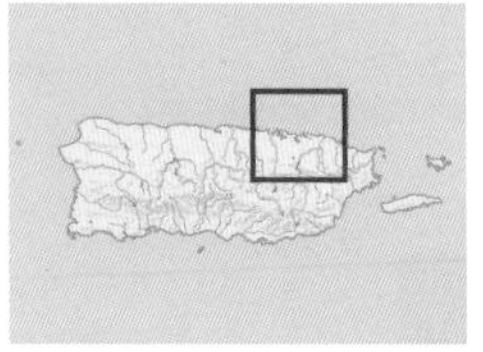

SAN JUAN AREA

THINGS TO DO: Learn about the stars, walk through an ancient fort, or take in a concert or a baseball game.

Bayamón

★ **Luis A. Ferré Science Park:** Fun and learning are combined in this park devoted to science. You can see stars in a planetarium, enjoy animals in a little zoo, and get a feel for flying in a flight simulator.

Guaynabo

★ **Caparra Ruins:** Walk around the ruins of the fort where Juan Ponce de León established Puerto Rico's first settlement in 1508.

Hiram Bithorn Stadium

Castillo de San Cristóbal

San Juan

★ **Castillo de San Cristóbal:** Walking down the narrow stone passageway to a stone sentry box, it is easy to imagine the life of a Spanish soldier at this colonial fort. Now part of the San Juan National Historic Site, it was the largest fort built by the Spanish in the Western Hemisphere.

★ **Museum of the Americas:** Since it opened in 1992, visitors to the Museo de las Américas in Old San Juan have been able to view a variety of art, from works created by Native people before Columbus arrived to those created by modern-day Latin American artists.

★ **Hiram Bithorn Stadium:** Catch a baseball game at this stadium, named for pitcher Hiram Bithorn, the first Puerto Rican baseball player to play on a Major League Baseball team. When seats are set up on the infield, 18,000 people can crowd in for concerts or other events.

★ **Pablo Casals Museum:** In 1957, the great Spanish cellist Pablo Casals made Puerto Rico his permanent home. The museum contains musical manuscripts and other memorabilia from this master.

★ **Roberto Clemente Coliseum:** From political rallies to world championship boxing matches, large events of all kinds are held in this stadium named in honor of Puerto Rico's beloved Major League Baseball star Roberto Clemente.

SEE IT HERE!

OLD SAN JUAN

Watch your step as you walk the uneven cobblestone streets of the original walled city of San Juan. In the place where Puerto Rico's Spanish colonial governors and other leaders once lived, you can now visit antique shops and boutiques—or just enjoy the old pastel-colored buildings with their balconies hanging over the narrow streets.

Luis Muñoz Rivera Park

★ **Luis Muñoz Rivera Park:** Take a stroll along the walkways in this seaside park that honors Puerto Rican statesman Luis Muñoz Rivera.

★ **Luis Muñoz Marín Foundation:** Take a short drive south of San Juan to the home of Luis Muñoz Marín, the first elected governor of Puerto Rico and one of the island's greatest heroes.

★ **Museo de Doña Fela:** The home of Felisa Rincón de Gautier, affectionately known as Doña Fela and the first woman to become mayor of San Juan, is now a museum in Old San Juan.

SEE IT HERE!

ARECIBO OBSERVATORY

Like a gigantic ear, the dish of the radio telescope at Arecibo on Puerto Rico's north coast listens for signals coming from deep space. A visit begins with a video about the observatory, and then you can tour the 3,500 square feet (325 sq m) of exhibits. From an observation platform, you'll have a great view of the 1,000-foot (305 m) radio telescope that discovered the first planets beyond our solar system.

Scenes in the movies *GoldenEye* and *Contact* were shot at Arecibo Observatory.

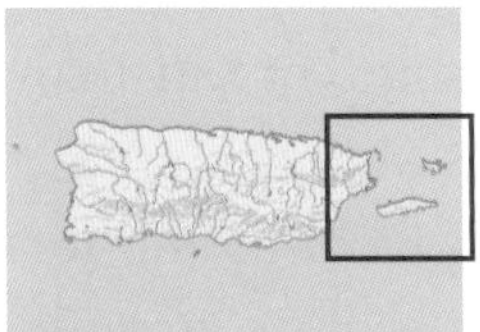

THE EAST

THINGS TO DO: Check out the wildlife on an island refuge, take a dip in the water off one of the world's most beautiful beaches, and see how wealthy plantation owners once lived.

Loíza

★ **Parroquia del Espíritu Santo y San Patricio:** Named for Saint Patrick and built in 1645, this is one of the oldest existing churches in Puerto Rico.

Luquillo Beach

★ **Luquillo Beach:** Offshore reefs keep the water calm and ideal for swimming or snorkeling at one of Puerto Rico's most beautiful beaches. Nearby, however, another Luquillo beach, nicknamed the Wall, has big waves that are great for surfing.

Culebra

★ **Culebra Natural Wildlife Refuge:** This wildlife refuge, managed by the U.S. Fish and Wildlife Service, covers the island of Culebra and 23 small islands nearby. The refuge is home to seabirds, shorebirds, lizards, and sea turtles, but no people. Visitors can hike, swim, watch wildlife, and even picnic—but everyone must pick up their trash to help preserve this ecosystem.

Guayama

★ **Casa Cautiño Museum:** This historic house, with ironwork that looks like white lace, is located on the plaza in Guayama. Tours offer a glimpse of how a wealthy plantation owner's family lived in the late 1800s.

Fajardo

★ **El Faro, the Lighthouse at Las Cabezas de San Juan State Park:** Every few seconds, the beacon flashes out across the sea from this gray and white lighthouse to signal ships approaching the northeastern tip of Puerto Rico, just as it has since 1880. The surrounding nature preserve has trails and boardwalks that go through seven different ecosystems.

Visitors to Las Cabezas de San Juan State Park

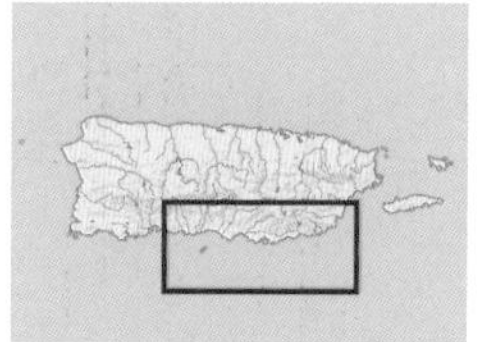

THE SOUTH

THINGS TO DO: Snorkel in the underwater world of tropical fish or take a nighttime boat ride into a bioluminescent bay.

Caja de Muertos

★ **Caja de Muertos Nature Reserve:** The clear waters around this island off the south coast of Puerto Rico offer snorkelers great views of tropical fish.

Coamo

★ **Church of San Blas de Illescas of Coamo:** Dating from 1661, this beautiful Roman Catholic Church was reconstructed in 1784.

★ **Coamo Historic Museum:** This big square building, also called the Picó Pomar Residence, was built in 1840 for a wealthy Spanish merchant. Today, it is a museum documenting the War of 1898 period.

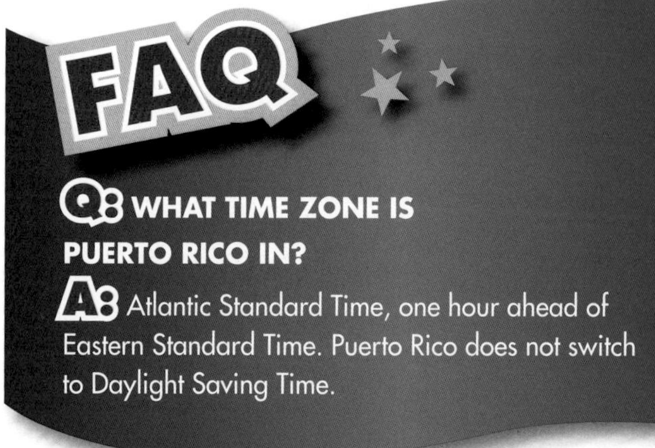

FAQ

Q8 WHAT TIME ZONE IS PUERTO RICO IN?

A8 Atlantic Standard Time, one hour ahead of Eastern Standard Time. Puerto Rico does not switch to Daylight Saving Time.

La Parguera Bioluminescent Bay

Between Ponce and Mayagüez

★ **La Parguera Bioluminescent Bay:** This bay is one of two Puerto Rican bays that glow at night with the light of microscopic organisms called dinoflagellates. The other bay is on Vieques. You can take a tour boat out into the bay and even do nighttime snorkeling for a close-up view of the eerie glow.

★ **Guánica Dry Forest:** Much of Puerto Rico is covered with tropical rain forest, but this dry forest is just the opposite. The 10,000 acres (4,047 ha) of desertlike land is home to some 600 plants and animals.

Ponce

★ **Ponce Museum of Art:** With more than 4,500 works of art, including paintings, sculptures, and photographs, this is one of the largest art museums in the Caribbean.

★ **Hacienda Buena Vista:** This living history museum shows visitors what life was like on a coffee plantation in the mid-1800s. You can walk among the coffee trees and then see waterfall-powered machines that stripped the pulp from coffee "cherries" to remove the bean inside. Learn how the beans were soaked, dried, and shelled before being bagged and shipped to roasters.

SEE IT HERE!

TIBES INDIAN CEREMONIAL CENTER

You can get a good idea of how Taínos lived before the Spanish arrived by visiting this reconstruction of a Native village on the site of an ancient burial ground. Graves, along with ball courts and rocks containing petroglyphs, were uncovered by floodwaters after a hurricane in 1975. A museum contains exhibits explaining the work of archaeologists who studied the site and the culture of the Native people who once lived here.

★ **Parque de Bombas:** This brightly striped building, located in the Ponce town square, served as the city's fire station for 100 years. It is now a museum that tells stories of fires such as the 1883 blaze that almost destroyed the city.

Parque de Bombas

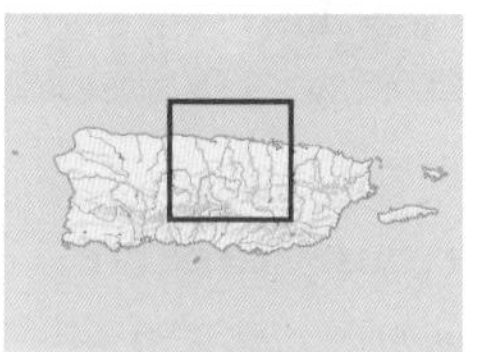

THE CENTRAL REGION

THINGS TO DO: Go kayaking, stroll through gardens, and marvel at an ancient Taíno ball court.

Barranquitas

★ **Birthplace of Luis Muñoz Rivera:** This modest, one-story wooden house was the birthplace of one of Puerto Rico's greatest political heroes, Luis Muñoz Rivera. It is now a museum.

Maricao

★ **Montoso Gardens:** Gorgeous tropical plants thrive within this private reserve in the mountains.

Utuado

★ **Caguana Ceremonial Ball Courts Site:** Built between 1200 and 1500, these ball courts, surrounded by carved stones, played an important role in Taíno life.

Jayuya

★ **Toro Negro Forest Reserve:** Straddling the cool, wet mountains of the Cordillera Central, this remote forest welcomes tent campers. You can also kayak on Matrullas Lake, one of Puerto Rico's highest lakes.

The observation tower at Toro Negro Forest Reserve

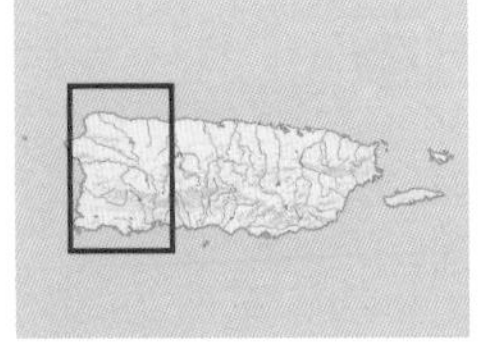

THE WEST

THINGS TO DO: Explore old churches, visit a working lighthouse, and descend into spectacular caves.

Añasco

★ **Parque Diversiones:** This amusement park claims the Caribbean's largest wave pool. Kids also love the medieval castle and haunted house. For grown-ups, there is an antiques museum.

San Germán

★ **San Germán Historic District:** Puerto Rico's second-oldest city dates from the time of early Spanish settlement. Most of the city's buildings date from different eras, including the 1800s.

Church of San Germán Auxerre

★ **Church of San Germán Auxerre:** This huge church on the city's main plaza began as a simple chapel in 1573, but now has a large crystal chandelier and a ceiling painted to create an optical illusion of 3-D boxes.

★ **Iglesia de Porta Coeli (Heaven's Gate Church):** The oldest existing church in the Americas dates from 1606. Restored by the Institute of Puerto Rican Culture, it has a museum with a large collection of antique santos, saints carved by Puerto Rican folk artists.

Cabo Rojo

★ **Los Morillos Light:** This lighthouse was built by the Spanish in 1881. It sits on a cliff high above the sea and to this day continues to guide ships to safety.

Los Morillos Light, Cabo Rojo

★ **Cabo Rojo National Wildlife Refuge:** Biologists are restoring this land, which used to include a ranch, to its original forest and grassland habitat. You can hike a 2-mile (3 km) interpretive trail through the refuge.

Camuy

★ **Camuy Caves:** The Camuy Caves, carved underground by the Camuy River about a million years ago, are one of the biggest cave systems in the Western Hemisphere. Guides take visitors to view spectacular natural columns and pillars.

Mayagüez

★ **Dr. Juan A. Rivero Zoo:** Spend some quality time with elephants, tigers, giraffes, and rhinoceroses at Puerto Rico's major zoo. Tropical birds fly freely around you in the enclosed bird sanctuary.

Exploring Camuy Caves

An iguana on Mona Island

★ **Mona Island:** The endangered Mona ground iguana, sea turtles, red-footed boobies, many seabirds, and other rare wildlife live on this island of cliffs, caves, and mangrove forests.

★ **Yagüez Theater:** The city's main performing arts center, this ornate palace of entertainment was declared a historic landmark in 1976.

Rincón

★ **Rincón Lighthouse Observation Park:** Spaniards built this park's Punta Higuero Lighthouse in the 1890s. Its electric beacon is as bright as 29,000 candles! The park is also a great place to watch for whales during winter months, especially February.

WRITING PROJECTS

Check out these ideas for creating a campaign brochure and writing you-are-there narratives. Or research the lives of famous Puerto Ricans.

118

ART PROJECTS

You can illustrate the commonwealth anthem, create a dazzling PowerPoint presentation, or learn about the official quarter and design your own.

119

TIMELINE

What happened when? This timeline highlights important events in the commonwealth's history—and shows what was happening in the United States at the same time.

122

GLOSSARY

Remember the Words to Know from the chapters in this book? They're all collected here.

125

FAST FACTS

Use this section to find fascinating facts about Puerto Rico's symbols, land area and population statistics, weather, sports teams, and much more.

126

SCIENCE, TECHNOLOGY, ENGINEERING, & MATH PROJECTS

PRIMARY VS. SECONDARY SOURCES

BIOGRAPHICAL DICTIONARY

RESOURCES

WRITING PROJECTS

Write a Memoir, Journal, or Editorial For Your School Newspaper!

Picture Yourself . . .

★ Preparing for a Taíno ceremony. As a young person, what clothing would you wear? What would your parents and other adults wear? Describe the sights and sounds of the event.

SEE: Chapter Two, page 30.

★ Taking part in the Cry of Lares. What has led to this struggle for independence from Spain, and why have you joined the fight? Describe the rebellion.

SEE: Chapter Four, pages 50–52.

Create an Election Brochure or Web Site!

Run for office! Throughout this book, you've read about some of the issues that concern Puerto Rico today. As a candidate for governor of Puerto Rico, create a campaign brochure or Web site.

★ Explain how you meet the qualifications to be governor of Puerto Rico.

★ Talk about the three or four major issues you'll focus on if you're elected.

★ Remember, you'll be responsible for Puerto Rico's budget. How would you spend the taxpayers' money?

SEE: Chapter Seven, page 88–89.

Create an interview script with a famous person from Puerto Rico!

★ Research various famous Puerto Ricans, such as Luis Muñoz Marín, Lola Rodríguez de Tió, Roberto Clemente, Luis Miguel Basteri, José Ferrer, and many others.

★ Based on your research, pick one person you would most like to talk with.

★ Write a script of the interview, perhaps in a question-and-answer format. What questions would you ask? How would this person answer? You may want to supplement this writing project with a voice-recording dramatization of the interview.

SEE: Chapters Four, Five, and Six, pages 53, 66, 79, 80, and 81, and the Biographical Dictionary, pages 133–137.

ART PROJECTS

Create a PowerPoint Presentation or Visitors' Guide

Welcome to Puerto Rico!

Puerto Rico is a great place to visit and to live! From its natural beauty to its historical sites, there's plenty to see and do. In your PowerPoint presentation or brochure, highlight 10 to 15 of Puerto Rico's fascinating landmarks. Be sure to include:

★ a map of the commonwealth showing where these sites are located

★ photos, illustrations, Web links, natural history facts, geographic stats, climate and weather, plants and wildlife, and recent discoveries

SEE: Chapter Nine, pages 106–115, and Fast Facts, pages 126–127.

Hummingbird feeds on a banana blossom

Illustrate the Lyrics to the Puerto Rico Commonwealth Anthem

("La Borinqueña")

Use markers, paints, photos, collages, colored pencils, or computer graphics to illustrate the lyrics to "La Borinqueña." Turn your illustrations into a picture book, or scan them into PowerPoint and add music.

SEE: The lyrics to "La Borinqueña" on page 128.

Research Puerto Rico's Quarter

From 1999 to 2008, the U.S. Mint introduced new quarters commemorating each of the 50 states in the order that they were admitted to the Union. In 2009, quarters were issued for Puerto Rico and Washington, D.C. Each quarter features a unique design on its reverse, or back.

★ Research the significance of the image. Who designed the quarter? Who chose the final design?

★ Design your own Puerto Rico quarter. What images would you choose for the reverse?

★ Make a poster showing the Puerto Rico quarter and label each image.

GO TO: www.factsfornow.scholastic.com. Enter the keywords **Puerto Rico** and look for the link to the Puerto Rico quarter.

SCIENCE, TECHNOLOGY, ENGINEERING, & MATH PROJECTS

Graph Population Statistics!

- ★ Compare population statistics (such as ethnic background, birth, death, and literacy rates) in Puerto Rico districts or municipalities.
- ★ In your graph or chart, look at population density and write sentences describing what the population statistics show; graph one set of population statistics and write a paragraph explaining what the graphs reveal.

SEE: Chapter Six, pages 72–74.

Create a Weather Map of Puerto Rico!

Use your knowledge of Puerto Rico's geography to research and identify conditions that result in specific weather events. What is it about the geography of Puerto Rico that makes it vulnerable to things such as hurricanes? Create a weather map or poster that shows the weather patterns over the commonwealth. Include a caption explaining the technology used to measure weather phenomena and provide data.

SEE: Chapter One, pages 14–15.

Track Endangered Species

Using your knowledge of Puerto Rico's wildlife, research which animals and plants are endangered or threatened.

- ★ Find out what the commonwealth is doing to protect these species.
- ★ Chart known populations of the animals and plants, and report on changes in certain geographic areas.

SEE: Chapter One, page 19.

PRIMARY VS. SECONDARY SOURCES

What's the Diff?

Your teacher may require at least one or two primary sources and one or two secondary sources for your assignment. So, what's the difference between the two?

★ **Primary sources are original.** You are reading the actual words of someone's diary, journal, letter, autobiography, or interview. Primary sources can also be photographs, maps, prints, cartoons, news/film footage, posters, first-person newspaper articles, drawings, musical scores, and recordings. By the way, when you conduct a survey, interview someone, shoot a video, or take photographs to include in a project, you are creating primary sources!

★ **Secondary sources are what you find in encyclopedias, textbooks, articles, biographies, and almanacs.** These are written by a person or group of people who tell about something that happened to someone else. Secondary sources also recount what another person said or did. This book is an example of a secondary source.

Now that you know what primary sources are—where can you find them?

★ **Your school or local library:** Check the library catalog for collections of original writings, government documents, musical scores, and so on. Some of this material may be stored on microfilm.

★ **Historical societies:** These organizations keep historical documents, photographs, and other materials.
Staff members can help you find what you are looking for. History museums are also great places to see primary sources firsthand.

★ **The Internet:** There are lots of sites that have primary sources you can download and use in a project or assignment.

TIMELINE

★ ★ ★

U.S. Events		Puerto Rico Events
	7000 BCE	
		c. 7000 BCE–3000 BCE Casimiroid people arrive from Central America.

c. 2000 BCE
Ortoiroid people arrive from South America.

c. 500 BCE
The Saladoid culture farms and makes pottery.

c. 600 CE
The Ostionoid culture builds plazas and ball courts.

Taíno shell necklace

c. 800
Arawak/Taíno people begin arriving.

Late 1400s
Caribs raid Taíno villages.

U.S. Events — 1492
Christopher Columbus and his crew sight land in the Caribbean Sea.

1493
Christopher Columbus lands on Puerto Rico.

1500

1509
Juan Ponce de León is named governor of the island.

1511
Taínos rebel against the Spanish.

1513
The first enslaved Africans arrive in Puerto Rico.

1539
Spaniards begin building El Morro.

Juan Ponce de León

U.S. Events		Puerto Rico Events
1565 Spanish admiral Pedro Menéndez de Avilés founds St. Augustine, Florida, the oldest continuously occupied European settlement in the continental United States.		**1598** English forces capture El Morro.
	1600	
1607 The first permanent English settlement in North America is established at Jamestown.		**1625** Dutch forces burn San Juan.
	1700	
1776 Thirteen American colonies declare their independence from Great Britain, marking the beginning of the Revolutionary War.		
	1800	
1812–15 The United States and Great Britain fight the War of 1812.		**1815** Spain allows Puerto Rico to begin trading with other nations.
1830 The Indian Removal Act forces eastern Native American groups to relocate west of the Mississippi River.		**1830** Large numbers of European immigrants begin arriving in Puerto Rico.
		1868 Rebels in favor of independence take control of Lares.
		1873 The Spanish government abolishes slavery.
1898 The United States gains control of Puerto Rico, the Philippines, and Guam after defeating Spain in the Spanish-American War.		**1898** The United States takes over Puerto Rico.
	1900	
1917–18 The United States engages in World War I.		**1917** Puerto Ricans become U.S. citizens.
1920 The Nineteenth Amendment to the U.S. Constitution grants women the right to vote.		**1920s** U.S. companies expand their sugar businesses in Puerto Rico.

U.S. Events

1929
The stock market crashes, plunging the United States more deeply into the Great Depression.

1941–45
The United States engages in World War II.

1950–53
The United States engages in the Korean War.

1964–73
The United States engages in the Vietnam War.

1991
The United States and other nations engage in the brief Persian Gulf War against Iraq.

2001
Terrorists hijack four U.S. aircraft and crash them into the World Trade Center in New York City, the Pentagon in Arlington, Virginia, and a Pennsylvania field, killing thousands.

2003
The United States and coalition forces invade Iraq.

Puerto Rico Events

1929
Some Puerto Rican women gain the right to vote.

1934
About 75 percent of Puerto Ricans are unemployed at the height of the Great Depression.

1937
Police and nationalist marchers clash at Ponce.

1941–45
Some 60,000 Puerto Ricans serve in World War II.

1948
Luis Muñoz Marín becomes Puerto Rico's first elected governor; Operation Bootstrap begins.

Luis Muñoz Marín

1952
Puerto Rico becomes a commonwealth.

1954
Puerto Rican nationalists attack the U.S. Congress.

1967
Puerto Rico holds its first referendum on commonwealth status.

1974
The Armed Forces of National Liberation (FALN) begin terrorist attacks.

2000

2000
Sila María Calderón is elected Puerto Rico's first female governor.

2011
Hurricane Irene strikes Puerto Rico.

GLOSSARY

anthropologists people who study the development of human cultures

archaeologists people who study the remains of past human societies

biotechnology the use of living organisms to develop new products such as foods and medicines

botanists scientists who study plants

cassava a starchy tropical root that looks somewhat like a big carrot

castes social classes that people are born into

conquistador one who conquers; specifically a leader in the Spanish conquest of the Americas

constitutional monarchy a government with a ruler whose power is regulated by law

duty-free without having to pay tax on exports or imports

erosion the gradual wearing away of rock or soil by physical breakdown, chemical solution, or water

exiled expelled from one's own country

famine a period of extreme food shortages and hunger

galleons heavy Spanish sailing ships from colonial times

incentives payments or other encouragement for greater investment, for example, by businesses

karst limestone regions that feature many caves and sinkholes

mestizos people of mixed Spanish and Indian heritage

missionaries people who try to convert others to a religion

nationalist a person who wants national independence

petroglyphs pictures carved or painted on stone

rain forest a dense forest of broad-leaved trees, usually found in warm, wet areas

referendum the people's vote on a particular issue

reforestation replenishing a forest by planting seeds or young trees

republic a government whose power belongs to the people

suffrage the right to vote

thatch a roof covering made of straw, palm leaves, or other plant material

FAST FACTS

Commonwealth Symbols

Official name Estado Libre Asociado de Puerto Rico, or Commonwealth of Puerto Rico
Origin of name From the Spanish for "rich port"
Commonwealth date July 25, 1952
Capital San Juan
Motto *Joannes Est Nomen Ejus* ("John Is Its Name")
Official bird Stripe-headed tanager
Official flower Puerto Rican hibiscus
Official song "La Borinqueña"
Official tree Ceiba

Commonwealth seal

Geography

Total area 5,325 square miles (13,792 sq km)
Land 3,424 square miles (8,868 sq km)
Water 1,901 square miles (4,924 sq km)
Inland water 68 square miles (176 sq km)
Coastal water 16 square miles (41 sq km)
Territorial water 1,817 square miles (4,707 sq km)
Latitude 18°00' N to 18°30' N
Longitude 65°15' W to 67°15' W
Highest point Cerro de Punta, 4,390 feet (1,338 m)
Lowest point Sea level along the Caribbean Sea
Largest city San Juan
Longest river Plata, 46 miles (74 km) long

Population

Population (2010 census)	3,725,789
Density (2010 census)	1,088 persons per square mile (418 per sq km)
Population distribution (2010 census)	94% urban, 6% rural
Ethnic distribution (2010 census)	Persons of Hispanic or Latino origin: 99.0% White persons: 0.7% Black persons: 0.1% Asian persons: 0.1%

Weather

Record high temperature	104°F (40°C) at Mona Island on July 2, 1996
Record low temperature	40°F (4°C) at Aibonito on March 9, 1911, at San Sebastián on January 24, 1966, and at Rincón on March 27, 1985
Average July temperature, San Juan	83°F (28°C)
Average January temperature, San Juan	78°F (26°C)
Average yearly precipitation, San Juan	56 inches (142 cm)

Commonwealth flag

COMMONWEALTH ANTHEM

★ ★ ★

"La Borinqueña"

Félix Astol Artés wrote the music to "La Borinqueña" in 1867, although he may have been altering a song that had been written in 1860 by Francisco Ramírez Ortíz. In 1868, Lola Rodríguez de Tió wrote lyrics for the song that supported independence from Spain. In 1903, Manuel Fernández Juncos wrote new lyrics for the song, and in 1952, the song was officially adopted as the anthem of the commonwealth.

Spanish lyrics

La tierra de Borinquén
donde he nacido yo,
es un jardín florido
de mágico fulgor.

Un cielo siempre nítido
le sirve de dosel
y dan arrullos plácidos
las olas a sus pies.

Cuando a sus playas llegó Colón;
Exclamó lleno de admiración;
"Oh!, oh!, oh!, esta es la linda
tierra que busco yo."

Es Borinquén la hija,
la hija del mar y el sol,
del mar y el sol,
del mar y el sol,
del mar y el sol,
del mar y el sol.

English translation

The land of Borinquen
where I was born.
It is a flowered garden
of magical brilliance.

A sky always clean
serves as a canopy.
And placid lullabies are given
by the waves at her feet.

When Columbus arrived at her beaches,
he exclaimed, full of admiration:
"Oh! Oh! Oh!
This is the beautiful land that I seek."

It is Borinquen the daughter,
the daughter of the sea and the sun.
of the sea and the sun,
of the sea and the sun,
of the sea and the sun,
of the sea and the sun!

NATURAL AREAS AND HISTORIC SITES

★ ★ ★

National Historic Sites

The National Park Service oversees and maintains one national historic site in Puerto Rico. The *San Juan National Historic Site* includes several forts—the oldest dating to 1539—built by the Spanish to defend against attackers. These forts—San Cristóbal, San Felipe del Morro, and San Juan de la Cruz, also called El Cañuelo—feature bastions, powder houses, and parts of the city wall.

National Forests

Puerto Rico is home to one national forest, *El Yunque National Forest,* which encompasses El Yunque rain forest in the Sierra de Luquillo. It is the only tropical rain forest in the U.S. national forest system.

La Mina Falls, El Yunque National Forest

SPORTS TEAMS

Puerto Rican Professional Baseball League

Lobos de Arecibo *(Arecibo Wolves)*
Criollos de Caguas *(Caguas Creoles)*
Gigantes de Carolina *(Carolina Giants)*
Indios de Mayagüez *(Mayagüez Indians)*
Leones de Ponce *(Ponce Lions)*
Atenienses de Manatí *(Manatí Athenians)*

Puerto Rican All-Star Game

CULTURAL INSTITUTIONS

Libraries

Biblioteca Madre María Teresa Guevara, or the Mother María Teresa Guevara Library, is at Sagrado Corazón University. It includes a Puerto Rican collection and a historical archive.

The *General Library* at the University of Puerto Rico's Mayagüez campus has several collections, including a Puerto Rico collection and a marine sciences special collection.

Museums

The *Casa Cautiño Museum* (Guayama) collection features Latin, Caribbean, and Puerto Rican art. There are also educational activities and a center for art documentation and investigation.

Museo de Arte Contemporáneo de Puerto Rico, or Museum of Contemporary Puerto Rican Art (San Juan), has an art collection by Puerto Rican, Caribbean, Central American, and South American artists.

Museo de las Américas, or Museum of the Americas (San Juan), used to be the home of Spanish troops. It now has permanent exhibits on popular art movements from North, Central, and South America, as well as the Caribbean.

The *Museum of Puerto Rican Music* (Ponce) has memorabilia of the region's music, along with exhibits on Indian, Spanish, and African instruments.

The *Ponce Museum of Art* has the Caribbean's most extensive art collection, ranging from works by European old masters to those of modern artists.

The *Puerto Rico Indian Museum* (San Juan) features objects made by Taínos, including various kinds of pots, stone and wooden ornaments, canoes, and arrows.

Performing Arts

Ballet Concierto de Puerto Rico (Santurce), founded in 1979, performs classical ballet and Latin dance on stages in Puerto Rico, elsewhere in the United States, and around the world in countries ranging from Cuba to Germany to Egypt.

The *Puerto Rico Symphony Orchestra* (San Juan) performs symphonies, operas, ballets, and pops concerts year-round.

Universities and Colleges

In 2011, Puerto Rico had 14 public and 48 private institutions of higher learning.

ANNUAL EVENTS

January–March

Carnival in Ponce (February)

Orange Festival in Las Marías (March)

Emancipation Day throughout the commonwealth (March 22)

April–June

Casals Festival in San Juan (mid-June)

Bomba y Plena Festival in Ponce (June)

Aibonito Flower Festival (June)

Eve of San Juan Bautista Day throughout the commonwealth (June 23)

San Juan Bautista Day throughout the commonwealth (June 24)

July–September

Barranquitas Artisans Fair (mid-July)

Loíza Festival (late July)

Festival of Santiago Apóstol in Loíza (July 25)

International Billfish Tournament in San Juan (September)

Inter-American Festival of the Arts in San Juan (September–October)

October–December

Columbus Day throughout the commonwealth (October 12)

Jayuya Indian Festival (November)

Discovery Day throughout the commonwealth (November 19)

Hatillo Festival of the Masks (late December)

Christmas celebrations throughout the commonwealth (late December)

Festival of Santiago Apóstol

BIOGRAPHICAL DICTIONARY

Íñigo Abbad y Lasierra (1745–1813), born in Spain, was a monk who became the first historian to write about Puerto Rico's history, culture, and wildlife. He lived in Puerto Rico from 1771 to 1778.

José Julián Acosta (1825–1891), born in San Juan, was a journalist and leader in the movement to abolish African slavery in the Americas.

José Miguel Agrelot (1927–2004), also known as Don Cholito, was a popular comedian and host of Puerto Rican radio and television shows. He was born in San Juan.

Pedro Albizu Campos See page 67.

Ricardo E. Alegría See page 31.

Miguel Algarín (1941–), born in Santurce, is a Puerto Rican poet and literature professor who cofounded the Nuyorican Poets Café in New York City.

Roberto Alomar (1968–), a native of Ponce, played second base for several Major League Baseball teams. During his career, he won 10 Gold Glove and four Silver Slugger awards.

Roberto Alomar

Francisco Arriví (1915–2007) was a poet and playwright known as the Father of the Puerto Rican Theater. Born in Santurce, he was also a poet and a radio host.

José Celso Barbosa (1857–1921), a doctor and politician born in Bayamón, worked to make Puerto Rico self-governing after the War of 1898. He founded the first pro-statehood party, the Republican Party, in 1899. He also served in Puerto Rico's senate from 1917 to 1921.

Luis Miguel Basteri See page 79.

Tomás Batista (1935–) of Luquillo, creator of *Monument to the Common Puerto Rican Countryman* and other works, is one of Puerto Rico's greatest sculptors.

Pura Belpré (1899–1982), a native of Cidra, was the first Puerto Rican librarian in New York City. She is best known for creating reading programs for the Spanish-speaking community. She also wrote children's books and translated Puerto Rican folktales that were published in the United States.

Ramón Emeterio Betances See page 51.

Hiram G. Bithorn (1916–1951), a pitcher born in Santurce, became the first Puerto Rican to play on a Major League Baseball team when he joined the Chicago Cubs in 1942.

Giannina Braschi (1953–) is a poet and novelist who writes in Spanish, English, and a blend of the two called Spanglish. She was born in San Juan and moved to New York City in 1977.

Julia de Burgos (1914–1953) was one of Puerto Rico's greatest poets and a supporter of rights for women and independence for Puerto Rico. She was born in Carolina.

Sila María Calderón

José M. Cabanillas (1901–1979) was an admiral in the U.S. Navy during World War II. He was awarded the Bronze Star Medal for his accomplishments during the Allied invasion of Europe. He was born in Mayagüez.

María Cadilla de Martínez (1884–1951) was an educator and writer, and one of the first women in Puerto Rico to earn a doctorate degree, or PhD. A native of Arecibo, she was active in social causes and a leader in the fight for women's voting rights.

Sila María Calderón See page 68.

José Campeche (1751–1809), a native of San Juan and son of a former slave, was one of Puerto Rico's first great painters. His works include religious paintings for churches and portraits.

Victor A. Carreño (1956–), raised in Guaynabo, became an engineer with the National Aeronautics and Space Administration (NASA) and invented the Single Frequency Multitransmitter Telemetry System, a low-cost method of delivering large amounts of data.

Rafael Carrión Sr. (1891–1964) was one of the founders of Banco Popular de Puerto Rico, the largest bank in Puerto Rico and the largest Hispanic bank in the United States. He was born in San Juan.

Pablo Casals (1876–1973) was a world-class Spanish cellist and conductor who settled in San Juan, his mother's birthplace, and founded the annual Casals music festival there.

Kimberly Casiano See page 101.

Orlando Cepeda (1937–) played first base for several Major League Baseball teams and was the second Puerto Rican elected to the National Baseball Hall of Fame. He was born in Ponce.

Rafael Cepeda See page 78.

Nitza Margarita Cintron (1950–), who was born in San Juan, is a NASA scientist who in 2004 became chief of the Space Medicine and Health Care Systems Office at the Johnson Space Center.

Roberto Clemente See page 81.

Elisa Colberg (1903–1988), born in Cabo Rojo, founded the Puerto Rican Girl Scouts in 1926. She led the organization for 27 years.

Rebekah Colberg (1918–1995), born in Cabo Rojo, is known as the Mother of Women's Sports in Puerto Rico. A graduate of the University of Puerto Rico, she was Puerto Rico's top tennis player for 14 years. In 1938, she won gold medals at the Central American and Caribbean Games in the discus and javelin-throw events.

Cayetano Coll y Toste (1850–1930), a native of Arecibo, was the official historian of Puerto Rico who wrote several books about the commonwealth.

Miriam Colon (1936–), a native of Ponce, is an actress and the founder of the Puerto Rican Traveling Theatre in New York City, where she is the director and a frequent performer in the group's productions.

Deirdre P. Connelly See page 99.

Angel Tomás Cordero Jr. (1942–) is a jockey who won more than 7,000 horse races, including three Kentucky Derby races. He was born in Santurce.

Rafael Cordero See page 75.

Justino Diaz (1940–) is a leading opera singer who has performed with companies such as the Metropolitan Opera in New York City and became director of Puerto Rico's Casals Festival. He was born in San Juan.

José de Diego (1866–1918), a native of Aguadilla, was a poet, journalist, and politician who supported Puerto Rican independence from the United States. His birthday is an official holiday in Puerto Rico.

José Feliciano

José Feliciano (1945–) is a singer and guitarist renowned as a classical, jazz, and rock 'n' roll musician. His "Feliz Navidad" is a popular Christmas song. He was born in San Juan and moved to New York City with his family when he was five years old.

Beatriz "Gigi" Fernández (1964–), born in San Juan, became one of the world's best tennis doubles players. She won 17 Grand Slam titles and two Olympic gold medals.

Manuel Fernández Juncos (1846–1928), a journalist and poet, wrote words to the tune "La Borinqueña," which in 1952 became Puerto Rico's official anthem. He was born in Spain but lived most of his life in Puerto Rico.

Luis Alberto Ferré (1904–2003), a native of Ponce, was an industrialist and politician who founded the New Progressive Party, which favors statehood. As this party's candidate, he became the third elected governor of the commonwealth.

Sixto A. Gonzalez (1965–) was the first Puerto Rican scientist to be named director of the Arecibo Observatory, a post he held from 2003 to 2006. He was born in Bayamón.

Rafaél Hernández Marín (1892–1965), a composer, wrote patriotic and Christmas music, conducted the Puerto Rican Symphony Orchestra, and founded Little League baseball in Puerto Rico. He was born in Aguadilla.

Eugenio María de Hostos (1839–1903), born in Mayagüez, was an educator and supporter of independence. He promoted education in the Dominican Republic, Peru, and elsewhere and argued for the education of women. His birthday is an official holiday in Puerto Rico.

Carmen Jovet (1944–), a native of Mayagüez, is a broadcast journalist and the first woman news anchor in Puerto Rico.

Beatriz "Gigi" Fernández

Raúl Juliá

Raúl Juliá (1940–1994), born in San Juan, was a stage and movie actor who won acclaim for his roles in the films *Kiss of the Spider Woman* and *The Addams Family*.

Enrique A. Laguerre Velez (1905–2005), of Moca, was nominated for a Nobel Prize in Literature in 1999. The novelist was also an advocate of environmental conservation.

Alfred "Butch" Lee (1956–), born in San Juan, was the first Puerto Rican to play in the National Basketball Association.

Ramón Lopez Irizarry (1897-1982), born in San Juan, was an agricultural professor at the University of Puerto Rico who found a way to create cream of coconut from the pulp of the coconut. He named the cream Coco Lopez. It is sold in grocery stores all over Europe and the United States and made him a multimillionaire.

René Marqués (1919–1979), a native of Arecibo, was a leading playwright, short-story writer, and novelist during the 1950s.

Concha Meléndez (1895–1983) was a teacher, writer, and critic of Hispanic American literature. She was born in Caguas.

Juan Morel Campos (1857–1896) was one of the finest composers of danza, a Puerto Rican form of classical dance music that can be either dreamy and romantic or spirited and festive. He was born in Ponce.

Rita Moreno

Rita Moreno (1931–), born Rosita Dolores Alverio in Humacao, is an actress, singer, and dancer. She is the only Puerto Rican to have won an Academy Award, an Emmy, a Grammy, and a Tony. Her first starring role was in the 1961 movie *West Side Story*, for which she won an Oscar.

Luis Muñoz Marín See page 66.

Luis Muñoz Rivera See page 86.

Antonia Novello

Antonia Novello (1944–), born in Fajardo, became the first female physician and the first Hispanic to serve as U.S. Surgeon General. In the post, which she held from 1990 to 1993, she campaigned against ads for alcohol and tobacco, especially those aimed at teenagers.

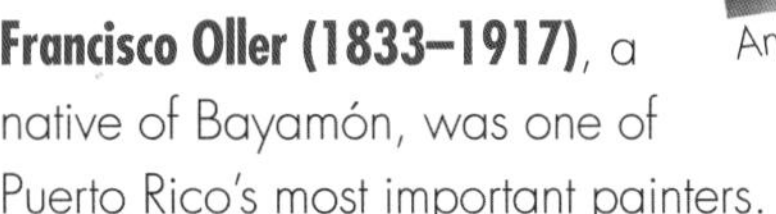

Francisco Oller (1833–1917), a native of Bayamón, was one of Puerto Rico's most important painters.

Choco Orta (1959–) is an actor and popular salsa singer and dancer who has recorded several Spanish language albums and also performed in concerts all over the Caribbean area, France, and the United States. She was born in Santurce.

Ernesto "Tito" Puente

Luis Palés Matos (1898–1959), from Guayama, was a poet who used African rhythms and words in his poetry and was known as one of the creators of the Afro-Antillean style of poetry.

Alfredo Wiechers Pieretti (1881–1964) was an architect who designed many buildings in his hometown of Ponce, including the one that now houses the Museum of Architecture. He often used elements of classical Greek and Roman architecture in his work.

Juan Ponce de León See page 35.

Ernesto "Tito" Puente (1923–2000), born in New York City's Spanish Harlem, brought Afro-Cuban music and Latin jazz to the attention of the world. His cultural contributions earned him a Smithsonian Medal.

Angel Ramos (1902–1960) was a newspaper publisher who established Telemundo, the Spanish-language television network in the United States. He was born in Manatí.

Felisa Rincón de Gautier See page 60.

Graciela Rivera (1921–2011), a native of Ponce, was a renowned opera singer. She moved to New York City after high school to study at the Juilliard School of Music and was the first Puerto Rican to sing a lead role at New York's Metropolitan Opera.

Ivan Rodriguez (1971–), known as Pudge, is a Major League Baseball catcher. He was born in Manatí.

Juan "Chi-Chi" Rodríguez (1935–), a professional golfer, was born in Rio Piedras. He won eight titles on the PGA Tour between 1963 and 1979 and then joined the Senior PGA Tour. In 1992, he became the first Puerto Rican inducted into the World Golf Hall of Fame.

Lola Rodríguez de Tió See page 53.

Pedro Rodriguez (1953–), director of NASA's Test Laboratory in the Engineering Directorate at Marshall Space Flight Center, invented a battery-operated lift chair to help people with arthritis in the knee. He was born in Bayamón.

Luis Rafael Sánchez (1936–), a native of Humacao, is an essayist, novelist, and one of Puerto Rico's greatest modern playwrights. His 1976 novel *Macho Camacho's Beat* sold well in both Spanish and English.

Arturo (Arthur) Alfonso Schomburg (1874–1938) grew up in San Juan and moved to New York City. He collected books and documents showing the importance of Africans in world and U.S. history, which became the Schomburg Collection of the New York Public Library, the world's largest collection of materials about people of African descent.

Agustín Stahl See page 21.

Manuel Gregorio Tavarez (1843–1883) was a composer and native of San Juan. He was called the Father of the Puerto Rican Danzas.

Manuel Zeno Gandía (1855–1930), who lived in Arecibo, was one of Puerto Rico's greatest novelists. His works include *La Charcha* (The Pond).

RESOURCES

BOOKS

Nonfiction

Aronson, Marc, and Marina Budhos. *Sugar Changed the World: A Story of Magic, Spice, Slavery, Freedom, and Science*. Boston: Clarion Books, 2010.

Gutner, Howard. *Puerto Rico*. New York: Children's Press, 2009.

Hernández, Roger E. *The Spanish-American War*. New York: Marshall Cavendish Benchmark, 2010.

Pelleschi, Andrea. *Juan Ponce de Leon*. New York: PowerKids Press, 2013.

Reis, Ronald A. *Christopher Columbus and the Age of Exploration for Kids: With 21 Activities*. Chicago: Chicago Review Press, 2012.

Rodriguez Gonzalez, Tania. *Roberto Clemente*. Broomall, Penn.: Mason Crest Publishers, 2013.

Worth, Richard. *Puerto Rico in American History*. Berkeley Heights, N.J.: Enslow Publishers, 2008.

Fiction

Delacre, Lulu. *Golden Tales*. Danbury, Conn.: Scholastic, 2001.

Jaffe, Nina. *The Golden Flower: A Taino Myth from Puerto Rico*. Houston: Piñata Books, 2005.

Ostow, Micol. *Emily Goldberg Learns to Salsa*. New York: Razorbill, 2007.

Ramirez, Michael Rose, and Margaret Sanfilippo. *The Legend of the Hummingbird: A Tale from Puerto Rico*. New York: Mondo Publishing, 1998.

Rohmer, Harriet, and Jesús Guerrero Rea. *Atariba and Niguayona: A Story from the Taíno People of Puerto Rico*. San Francisco: Children's Book Press, 1988.

FACTS FOR NOW

Visit this Scholastic Web site for more information on Puerto Rico:
www.factsfornow.scholastic.com
Enter the keywords **Puerto Rico**

INDEX

★ ★ ★

Page numbers in *italics* indicate illustrations.

AUTHOR'S TIPS AND SOURCE NOTES

★ ★ ★

While researching this book, I found *The History of Puerto Rico: From the Spanish Discovery to the American Occupation*, by R. A. Van Middeldyk, to be very helpful. A number of books—including *Economic History of Puerto Rico*, by James L. Dietz, and *Puerto Rico: A Political and Cultural History*, by Arturo Morales Carrión—cover the story of Puerto Rico from Spanish colonial to modern times. When researching a state, commonwealth, or country, don't overlook the various tourism boards. The official Puerto Rico Tourism Company works with the commonwealth government to produce excellent print and online information about places of interest.

Photographs ©: age fotostock: 112 (Jean Du Boisberranger), 108 top, 110 (Ken Welsh), 114 top (Morales); akg-Images, London/ Francois Guenet: 4 top center, 23 bottom, 30, 122 top; Alamy Images: cover inset (Anton Gorbov), 19, 120 (Kevin Schafer), 22 top, 23 top left (M. Timothy O'Keefe), 27 (Melvyn Longhurst), 33 bottom, 40 (Mira), 29 (Nik Wheeler), 111, 113 top (Robert Fried), 119 right (Tom Grundy), 56 bottom (Westend61); Animals Animals/Viola's Photo Visions Inc.: 113 bottom; AP Images: 24, 108 bottom (Andres Leighton), 80 top (Harry Harris), 57 top right, 63 (Jack Delano/Library of Congress), 50 (John McConnico), 14 (Marta Lavandier), 84, 85 left (Ricardo Arduengo), 71 right, 80 bottom, 130 bottom (Ricardo Figueroa), 135 left (Stephen Chernin), 66 bottom, 67, 81, 133; Art Resource, NY/Snark: 37; Bridgeman Art Library International Ltd., London/New York: 45 top right, 49 (Jean Baptiste Labat/Bibliotheque Nationale, Paris, France/Lauros/Giraudon), 26 top (Ken Welsh/Caguana Ceremonial Park, Puerto Rico), 42 (Museo Nacional de Historia, Mexico City, Mexico/Giraudon), 38 (Royal Commonwealth Society, London, UK); Corbis Images: 54, 57 bottom, 60, 61, 62, 66 top, 124 (Bettmann), 31 bottom (Gianni Dagli Orti), 68, 134 (Jason Szenes), 22 bottom, 26 bottom (JupiterImages/Brand X), 136 top right (Mitchell Gerber), 101 bottom (Onne van der Wal), 9 right, 18 bottom (Stephen Frink), 136 bottom (Thais Llorca/epa), 13 (Tom Bean), 132 (Tony Arruza), 56 top, 57 top left; Danita Delimont Stock Photography: 97 right, 105 (Ellen Clark), 4 top left, 17 bottom, 116 top, 119 left (Rolf Nussbaumer); Dave G. Houser/HouserStock, Inc.: 76, 78; DK Images/Peter Dennis: 23 top right, 28; Dreamstime/Andrii Deviatov: back cover; Courtesy of Eli Lilly and Company/Archivo: 99; Everett Collection, Inc./Jack Delano: 20; Ford Motor Company/Casiano Communications: 101 top; Getty Images: 75 (Christian Science Monitor), 134 right (Clive Brunskill), 79 (Ethan Miller), 64 (Gordon Parks), 96, 96 left (Steve Dunwell), 70, 71 left (Tim Draper), cover (Wendell Metzen); Inmagine: 45 bottom, 85 right, 94, 123, 127; iStockphoto: 116 bottom, 130 top (David Freund), 128 (Vladislav Lebedinski); John Elk III: 21, 129; Kobal Collection/Picture Desk/Jordi Socias/Fandango/Canal+/SGAE: 137 bottom; Library of Congress: 53, 86 top (Hispanic Division/Puerto Rican Institute of Culture), 44 bottom, 51; Lonely Planet Images/John Elk III: 86 bottom; Mary Evans Picture Library: 43; Minden Pictures: 17 top (Gerry Ellis), 18 top (Heidi & Hans-Jurgen Koch); National Archives and Records Administration: 58; National Geographic Stock: 115 bottom (David Boyer), 31 top (Stephanie Maze); North Wind Picture Archives: 44 top, 45 top left, 55; Omni-Photo Communications/KPA: 136 top left; Photo Researchers, NY/George Haling: 98; Photolibrary: 109 top (Barry Winiker/Index Stock Imagery), 121 (Somos Images), 114 bottom (Wendell Metzen/Index Stock Imagery); Photoshot/Jean-Marc Lecerf/World Pictures: 10; Reuters/Ana Martinez: 89; Robert Fried Photography: 77; Robertstock.com: 109 bottom (Alec Conway/TIPS), 82 bottom, 83 bottom (Foodcollection), 82 top (Isabelle Rozenbaum); Superstock, Inc.: 4 bottom, 83 top (Brand X), 8, 9 (Wolfgang Kaehler); The Granger Collection, New York: 4 top right, 32 top, 32 bottom, 33 top right, 33 top left, 35, 36, 39, 46, 48, 122 bottom; The Image Works: 115 top (Avampini/VW), 90 (Jeff Greenberg), 103 (Katherine McGlynn), 69 (Sven Martson); Vector-Images.com: 95, 126.

Maps by Map Hero, Inc.